What People Are Saying About

Against the Vortex

Like a pastry chef who can MacGyver a five-star dessert out of a Twinkie or a Jell-O packet, Anthony Galluzzo confects something special from the unlikeliest of industrial products: the 1974 Connery-Rampling vehicle *Zardoz*. His secret ingredient is "critical aquarianism," a counter-modernist blend of radical tech critique and ebullient degrowth, and it carries the flavor of radical, careful thinking. Readers who rail among and against the machines of the world will savor this book, even in the waste and ruin.

Matt Tierney, author of *Dismantlings: Words Against Machines in the American Long Seventies*

Few people have seen the 1974 film *Zardoz*. And even those who have will likely remember little more than Sean Connery running around the desert with a space gun, wearing only a red diaper and thigh-high leather boots. Anthony Galluzzo, however, has watched this camp cult classic very closely and has drawn many fascinating lessons from the psychedelic wreckage. Indeed, Galluzzo has a genius for using neglected and misunderstood cultural texts as a prism for fiercely independent ideological critique, as well as opportunities for sketching promising political paths not taken. In this case, the author offers the intriguing prospect of a "critical aquarianism": a concept and orientation that recovers the less compromised utopian energies of the past in order to fight the more Promethean techno-utopias of the present (and ominous near-future). Quite a feat! Indeed, who knew that Sean Connery was carrying quite so much inside that lurid red diaper?

Dominic Pettman, Professor of Media and New Humanities at The New School, cultural theorist, and author of *Creaturely Love: How Desire Makes Us More and Less Than Human*

Against the Vortex is a delightful and surprisingly hopeful read. In the guise of film criticism, Anthony Galluzzo has laid out the foundation of a biocentric utopianism that re-directs our political imaginations away from technological delusion and towards what is truly possible. It turns out I'm a critical Aquarian, and you'll probably discover that you are, too.
Rhyd Wildermuth, author of *Here Be Monsters: How to Fight Capitalism Instead of Each Other*

AGAINST THE VORTEX

ZARDOZ AND DEGROWTH UTOPIAS IN THE SEVENTIES AND TODAY

Anthony Galluzzo

London, UK
Washington, DC, USA

CollectiveInk

First published by Zer0 Books, 2023
Zer0 Books is an imprint of Collective Ink Ltd.,
Unit 11, Shepperton House, 89 Shepperton Road, London, N1 3DF
office@collectiveinkbooks.com
www.collectiveinkbooks.com
www.zero-books.net

For distributor details and how to order please visit the 'Ordering' section
on our website.

Paperback ISBN: 978 1 80341 662 5
eBook ISBN: 978 1 80341 666 3
PCN: 2023945509

A CIP catalogue record for this book is available from the British Library.

Design credit(s): Lapiz Digital

UK: Printed and bound by CPI Group (UK) Ltd, Croydon, CR0 4YY
Printed in North America by CPI GPS partners

We operate a distinctive and ethical publishing philosophy in
all areas of our business, from our global network of authors to
production and worldwide distribution.

CONTENTS

Once,

I was afraid of dying
In a field of dry weeds.
But now,

All day long I have been walking among damp fields,
Trying to keep still, listening
To insects that move patiently.

Perhaps they are sampling the fresh dew that gathers slowly
In empty snail shells

And in the secret shelters of sparrow feathers fallen on the
earth.
— James Wright, "I Was Afraid of Dying"

As we know that blood is birth, agony breaks open doors, as we
can bend, graciously, beneath burdens, undermine like rain, or
earthworms, as our cries yield to the cries of the newborn, as we
hear the plea in the voices around us, not words of passion or
cunning, discount anger or pride, grow strong in our own strength,
women's alchemy, quick arms to pull down walls, we liberate out
of our knowledge, labor, sucking babes, we liberate, and nourish,
as the earth
— Diane di Prima, Revolutionary Letter #44

In all those houses the backward-head people lived. They had
electrical wires in their ears, and were deaf. They smoked tobacco
day and night, and were continually making war. He tried to get
away from the war by going on, but it was everywhere they lived,
and they lived everywhere. He saw them hiding and killing each
other. Sometimes the houses burned for miles and miles. But there
were so many of those people that there was no end to them.
— Ursula Le Guin, from *Always Coming Home*

In Memory of S.B. (June 10, 1973-April 21, 1997).

With Gratitude to D.P.

For A.T.

I
INTRODUCING *ZARDOZ*

John Boorman's 1974 cult film oddity, *Zardoz*, is now mostly remembered for star Sean Connery's high-camp red-leather outfit (Fig 2) and the eponymous flying stone head (Fig 1) who inaugurates the movie's narrative action in declaring, "The gun is good. The penis is evil. The penis shoots seeds and makes new life to poison the Earth with a plague of men, as once it was. But the gun shoots death and purifies the Earth of the filth of the Brutals. Go forth and kill. Zardoz has spoken."[1] Although the film was a commercial and critical disaster, no less a figure than a young Fredric Jameson thought the work significant enough to write on it at length soon after its release, and in a way that looks forward to his later ruminations on ideology and utopia, while Boorman himself considered the story important enough to put into "novel form"—after the film's release and box office failure—in response to those "ghosts that stalked the Celtic twilight" and "pressed this strange vision of the future upon me."[2]

Zardoz's baroque plot, which Boorman and co-writer, Bill Stair, clarify and elaborate in their curious 1974 novelization, takes place in 2293 on an Earth devastated by nuclear war or ecological catastrophe or both. The Brutal human majority—mostly mutated due to radiation—are kept in check by the Exterminators, led by Zed (Connery). These Exterminators alternately kill and enslave the Brutals—forcing them to grow corn, for instance—at the behest of Zardoz, the flying stone head who dispenses weapons alongside imperatives to his Exterminator acolytes. Zed, suspecting Zardoz is not all that he appears to be, slips into the flying stone head hidden among the Exterminators' regular agricultural tribute to discover that his god is in fact an airship piloted by an elaborately dressed human figure. (Boorman's false sky god was inspired by William Blake's depiction of Nebuchadnezzar and his poem "To Nobodaddy"; Blake is one significant link between the visionary romanticism of the 1790s and the countercultures of the Sixties and Seventies.)[3] Zed shoots this figure, and the head goes down as a result, crash-landing in a lush, high-tech oasis known as the Vortex.

This event inaugurates Zed's journey as he learns that the world— or the Outlands outside the Vortex—is run by the Eternals. This technologically advanced human elite, working in tandem with a supercomputer called the Tabernacle, possess seemingly godlike powers that include ersatz immortality as the Tabernacle repeatedly downloads each Eternal's consciousness into new bodies grown from the genetic codes it stores and controls. The Eternals have for this reason dispensed with sexual intercourse, which they consider an unnecessary atavism, in line with Enlightenment-era perfectibilist William Godwin's prediction that the triumph of reason would bring sexless immortality to humankind. The Eternals manage the Brutal majority by way of the stone head and their Exterminator devotees. The Exterminators therefore unwittingly enforce the Eternals' murderous population and resource management imperatives against their fellow Brutals. We also learn that the Eternals once sought to leave the planet to join other Eternal space colonies. The Tabernacle developed the technology behind the Vortex's flying phony sky god for the purposes of interplanetary travel while maintaining the Brutal population as seed material for a space colonization project, until that project collapsed.

Zed brings discord to the Vortex, as informal leader Consuella (Charlotte Rampling) puts the "animalistic" Outlander on display for the ostensible purpose of scientific experiment. She, for instance, scans Zed's consciousness, forcing him to relive his past, as his mostly violent memories are projected onto a screen for an audience of Eternals: a clever variation on the flashback that implicitly identifies *Zardoz*'s largely Anglo-American audiences with the film's Immortal overlords. Consuella "tests" Zed's sexual function, which in turn discomfits and awakens the dormant sexual desires of her Eternal audience (and ultimately Consuella herself, at least by the film's end). Perhaps this is why Consuella wants to kill Zed immediately, setting her against May (Sarah Kestelman). May, supported by the majority, prefers that Zed live, at least temporarily, for the purpose of further study.

Zed is made to play servant to Friend (John Alderton) during this stay of execution. It is Friend who first exposes Zed to the rot at the heart of Eternal life—the ennui and imbecility that come from post-Singularity techno-immortalism—dramatically depicted in a growing subpopulation of Apathetics. Friend also introduces his Exterminator "slave" to the Renegades. The Renegades are Eternals who, in violating the Tabernacle-enforced Eternal consensus around norms of enlightened behavior and belief, are punished through expedited aging. Which is one reason these geriatric Immortal renegades want nothing so much as to die.

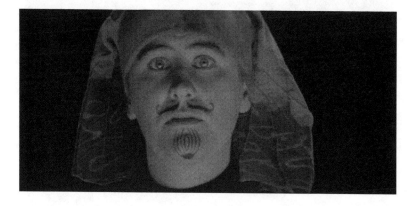

Friend himself is ultimately punished as a Renegade, after he vocally attacks the Vortex and its system, even as Zed learns that he was specifically engineered by a group of dissident Eternals to undo the Tabernacle and bring the "gift of death" to the Immortals, whose power and immortality stem from the immiseration of the Outlands. These dissident Eternals include Friend and Arthur Frayn (Niall Buggy), the figure piloting the Zardoz head who Zed only apparently dispatches at the start of the film (and it is Frayn's odd quasi-Shakespearian prologue that opens the film). Frayn, whose remit includes the management of the Outlands, designed the flying stone head as a form of social control after the wizard-trickster in L. Frank Baum's *Wizard of Oz*; hence *Zard-oz*. (In one significant flashback, we learn that it was Zed's apparently accidental discovery of the children's novel during a raid on a Brutal encampment that awakens his skepticism regarding the head, all according to Frayn's plan.)

Zed is a catalyst, designed by one segment of the Eternals' intent on dissolving the Vortex. The final act of the film is consequently occupied by a civil war among the Eternals, as Consuella and her loyalists seek to capture and kill Zed and his new dissident Eternal allies, who include May, Friend, a reconstituted Frayn, and Avelow, the Eternal seeress who sees that the outsider will put an end to the Vortex. Even Consuella eventually embraces Zed's mission. The Eternal matriarchs "impregnate" Zed with the collective knowledge of the Vortex, even as he literally impregnates them: "They would guide him and bathe him in their knowledge, so that their minds would mix through the touching of their skins. And as he mated so would they pass back to him their own seeds of information that would grow in him, as the life he transmitted would grow in them."[4]

Boorman's novelistic description falls far short of his film's exuberant exercise in cinematic psychedelia—achieved by cinematographer Geoffrey Unsworth "in camera," using old-fashioned techniques, such as projecting images onto invisible glass—which bears comparison to other visionary films of the time, such as Alexander Jodorowski's *El Topo*, Sergei Parajanov's *The Color of Pomegranates*, and Unsworth's own work in Stanley Kubrick's *2001*. In the case of the "impregnation" scene, for example, Unsworth projected various images of Western art and thought onto "the faces and half-naked bodies of May and her followers, while Zed, who is at first passive and finally overwhelmed, absorbs the information. The complex look of the scene was deceptively simple (but time-consuming) to achieve and required 'two 16mm film projectors and a stills projector' to beam the various images onto the actors."[5] The seeming discrepancy between the film's visual surfeit and its narrative led some critics of the time to confess their own cognitive dissonance: "My response to *Zardoz* is paradoxical. I admire the visual artistry but reject the fascist vision."[6] For critic Kinder, this "fascist vision" consists of what she took to be Boorman's retrograde gender politics—which I will address in the concluding section of the book. More than his novelization, Boorman's response to these criticisms better conveys the visual texture of the "impregnation" scene: "Somebody said to me that what it comes down to in the end is that Zed has to bang some sense into these women, which is the exact opposite to what happens because actually they bang sense into him, don't they? In the scene where they give him their knowledge, they are the sexual aggressors and he's totally passive."[7]

In the film's denouement, Zed destroys the techno-magical crystal that contains the Tabernacle's intelligence and power—and with it the Eternals' prosthetic superhumanity—in a hallucinatory shootout sequence that invokes the well-known hall-of-mirrors conclusion to Orson Welles's *Lady From Shanghai* (1947), albeit in a characteristically surreal register. Up until this point, this master crystal functioned as server (and more) for the individual crystal transmitters that, as we see over the course of the film, telepathically bound the Eternals to each other by way of the Tabernacle, allowing them to "ascend" through various levels of collective consciousness in a hippie modernist adumbration of a still-nascent "world wide web." Zed ultimately learns that the (now Renegade) scientists who first devised Tabernacle and Vortex ostensibly did so to preserve civilization and the sum total of human knowledge, but more than that. The film's technocrat wizards also sought to achieve human perfection. What perfection and whose?

Boorman's fable exemplifies that strand of early Seventies countercultural thinking that challenged the hypermodernist vision that drove both US capitalism and Soviet state socialism. This vision, which I will further explore over the course of my argument, encompasses familiar elements of Western, and typically industrial capitalist, ideology. A non-exhaustive list of these elements would include: a belief in historical progress, defined in entirely Western and industrial terms and largely identified with scientific-technological development no matter the cost; a Promethean embrace of endless material growth and a corresponding refusal of biophysical limits and human self-limitation; a reified and hierarchical split between mind and body, human beings and a natural world reconceived as standing reserve or "ecosystem services" for human use and manipulation. Here is anthropologist James C. Scott's "high modernist ideology" with its drive toward the abstraction, quantification, and total control of a messy and recalcitrant world. While we should not deny the benefits of modernity, up to a point, we can now see the consequences of this ideology and the socioeconomic system it underwrites in the form of planetary ecological collapse. "Hypermodernism" is my shorthand for those extreme and explicitly transcendental manifestations of an ostensibly secular modernist mindset that usually come to the fore in moments of crisis, exemplified by the various "futurisms" that mark the intellectual (and political) history of the modern era from Russian cosmism to Silicon Valley transhumanism.

The deliberately ridiculous elements of *Zardoz*—which include Connery in a thong, playing a murderous barbarian-enforcer killing other barbarians on behalf of a godlike techno-scientific elite, in a defamiliarizing echo of the James Bond plots for which Connery was famous at the time—are very much to the point here. Or so I will argue in counterpoint to the new, yet decidedly nostalgic futurism that dominates recent left-inflected cultural commentary and political analysis, often in a manner indistinguishable from libertarian and alt-right Singularitarianism or Long Termism. Under labels such as "left accelerationism" and "fully automated luxury communism," we can detect an ironically backward-looking desire for those high-modernist "lost futures" of the twentieth century, to invoke cultural critic Mark Fisher,[8] that supposedly offer us the lineaments of a better world.

In *Four Futures: Life after Capitalism*, *Jacobin* magazine editor Peter Frase outlines four speculative futures ranging from a glorious high-tech, post-work cornucopia to a post-collapse eco-dystopia Each of these "futures" is refracted through a science fiction text—film, TV show, or novel—as Frase combines social analysis and interpretive reverie, or what he calls "social science fiction." Frase's preferred techno-utopia is Gene Roddenberry's *Star Trek*—a fetish for yet another generation of fans who see in this pop-modernist artifact of the Space Age a blueprint for a "Star Trek socialism"—which he counterposes to the dark premonitions depicted in Kim Stanley Robinson's *California Trilogy* or Orson Scott Card's *Ender's Game*.[9]

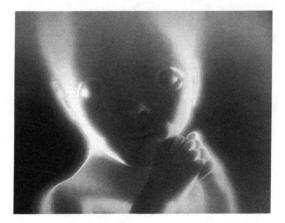

Star Trek and the space operas that define postwar science fiction, both on the page and on-screen, are very much the object of Boorman's satire and pastiche in this surrealist film of ideas. (And the film is "sureralist" in a specific sense insofar as Boorman explores the unconscious psychosexual drives behind various science fictional "dreams of reason.") It is in these science fictions that we can see the rational-empiricist yet implicitly religious logic of modernity—for example, the religion of Progress, whereby history proceeds in necessary stages toward some predetermined Enlightenment endpoint—take explicitly religious hypermodernist form. Hence those Promethean dreamworks that depict the achievement of traditionally Christian or Gnostic ends—such as immortality, the transcendence of our embodied natural world, and the flight to heaven—by way of techno-scientific means.

This postwar hypermodernist vision is best exemplified (if in a knowing and perhaps ironic way) by Stanley Kubrick's 1969 film adaptation of Arthur C. Clarke's *2001: A Space Odyssey*. Kubrick's film, in repurposing space opera as a vehicle for abstract philosophical speculation on human origins and ends, provides the template for Boorman's own kaleidoscopic work. And *2001* is a recognizable influence on *Zardoz*—from cinematographer Unsworth, who also shot Kubrick's film, to the prominence of Beethoven's *Seventh Symphony* in David Munrow's score to the film's startling, even psychedelic, juxtapositions of primitive and futuristic milieux. But while *2001* self-consciously strives to elevate the popular science fiction film in underlining the idea of Western techno-science as religious project, *Zardoz* deflates these same hypermodernist dreams. Frayn himself announces in the prologue, appended to the film after a test-screen audience's initial incomprehension, that the fable to follow is "rich in irony and deeply satirical."[10] As one early and perceptive critic noted: "The film, which has inevitably been compared to Kubrick's *2001: A Space Odyssey*, seems to me much closer in general narrative spirit to movies like Fellini's *Satyricon*."[11]

I accordingly offer my reading of *Zardoz* as another sort of "social science fiction," one that is also archaeological, as I excavate a broader post-Sixties movement and current of thought—decelerationist, neo-Luddite, and counter-modernist—of which *Zardoz* was a part. This constellation was an important forerunner of degrowth, among other contemporary movements, that see in a certain developmentalist imperative that defines the modernization process the root of our current social, ecological, and existential crises.

Rather than recovering some incomplete project of modernity, then equating that project with the utopian impulse, I will argue that *Zardoz*—and its moment—challenges us to think utopia and limits together in a way that is inexplicable to those "*Star Trek* socialists" who cannot distinguish freedom and flourishing from Faustian final frontiers; in fact, *Zardoz* is very much a Swiftian riposte to *Star Trek* and the Promethean fever dreams of postwar science fiction. Hence the essay that follows is not so much a call for yet another "future" as it is a plea to pull the emergency brake, as heterodox Marxist cultural critic and philosopher Walter Benjamin counseled in the face of his own catastrophic moment: it is only after the "future" and among the ruins that we will build our necessarily imperfect utopias.

II

THE YOUNG JOHN BOORMAN AND HIS CONTEXTS: CRITICAL AQUARIANISM AND THE ZARDOZIAN MOMENT

Boorman is an English filmmaker who found mainstream success in Hollywood with the Lee Marvin vehicle *Point Blank* (1967) and then *Deliverance* (1972). He moved between the US and British film industries, shifting from relatively straightforward narrative films and idiosyncratic works—like *Leo the Lion* (1970), *Zardoz,* and *The Heretic* (1977), a much-maligned followup to William Friedkin's *The Exorcist.* These last films straddle the line between experimentalism and kitsch. In a 2015 interview, an older Boorman described himself during this time as "very much a left-wing Marxist. I was determined to put an end to this nonsense of the British Empire."[12] If we are to take him at his word, he was a very peculiar Marxist, who combined left-wing and anti-colonial politics with an avid interest in myth and legend—particularly the grail mythos, Jungian psychology, ecology, and a Luddite skepticism toward a toxic technosphere at odds with the technocentric, narrowly materialist, and militantly modernist outlooks of most orthodox Marxists.

Like such artist-contemporaries as Ursula Le Guin and Russel Hoban, Boorman exemplified a certain strand of the late-Sixties counterculture that defined itself through the rejection of ossified modernist orthodoxies. We can see in the variegated output of these figures and various other intellectual fellow travelers—such as Norman O. Brown, Ivan Illich, Theodore Roszak, Maria Mies, Barry Commoner, Andre Gorz, Paul Shepard, Paul Irwin Thomas, or even the young James Lovelock and Lynn Margulis—a deliberately eclectic program that combined individual exploration and communal spirit, folk traditionalism and avant-garde experimentation, and finally, reason and imagination in the vein of the first-generation Romantics at their most radical. Here was a critical Aquarianism encompassing neo-Luddism and a revisionist utopianism within limits—which I will discuss further below—whose advocates often positioned themselves against other Aquarianisms of the time, ranging from therapeutic cults of the self to hippie modernist cults of technology to cults plain and simple.

Boorman accordingly made an abortive attempt to adapt counterculture favorite J.R.R. Tolkien's *The Lord of the Rings*, for which he failed to secure funding, prior to embarking on *Zardoz*, with its signature combination of fantasy and science fictional elements. Tolkien's epic, animated by its author's radical traditionalism, appealed to the anti-modernist elements of the counterculture during this period. Boorman was specifically drawn to Tolkien's source materials, especially the quest narrative and Merlin archetype that respectively inform the protagonist Frodo's journey and the figure of Gandalf. Boorman would later tackle the Arthurian mythos in his *Excalibur*, but it was his dissatisfaction with Tolkien's vision and its easy traditionalism that inspired *Zardoz* and its ambiguities, as he explained in a subsequent interview: "the more I worked on the Tolkien, the more it diminished—in the end, Tolkien always really avoids the big issues."[13] One such big issue is the question of technology and its unintended consequences, perhaps allegorized in the form of the ring at the center of Tolkien's fantasy.

Technology, itself, is an almost meaningless abstraction covering everything from the simple tools and language use that constitute human beings in their "original technicity," after Bernard Stiegler, to the complex industrial and capitalist megatechnical systems that, from the vantage point of the 1970s, were very much at the center of the twentieth century and its string of catastrophes, stretching from the World Wars through a then-contemporaneous Southeast Asia atrocity and what were the first signs of the planetary ecological breakdown we are grappling with today.

The standard Marxist answer to this question is that the problem does not reside in the technology, or forces of production, but in the social system, or relations of production, in which those forces are embedded; but the catastrophic twentieth century arguably tells us another story, as heterodox Western Marxists from Benjamin to Hebert Marcuse argued in the face of Nazism and Stalinism, on the one hand, and the capitalist West, on the other: united in their pursuit of industrialized mass murder and the totally administered world despite their differences. This same dissident Marxism significantly shaped the Sixties-era's new left, for which Marcuse, ensconced in a professorship at UC Santa Barbara, was a guru.

But even these dissident Marxisms harbored modernist hopes, as another, slightly later current of neo-Luddite thinkers—represented in the works of Ivan Illich, John Noble, and Langdon Winner—noted in arguing that ruling-class imperatives and hierarchical structures of command are embedded in the very architectures of our complex socio-technological systems, from the automated assembly line to the medical-industrial complex and a then-emergent DARPANET (i.e., the internet). Meanwhile, theorists of underdevelopment focused on how these systems are built through uneven and exploitative forms of neocolonial extraction and exchange. Boorman was somewhat aware of these issues at the time, as he reveals in a more recent reflection on his film and its contexts:

"In the early Seventies, the rich were already getting richer and the poor were getting poorer. The rich were also living longer, with better access to resources. My idea was to extend that process into the future, to where the rich have achieved immortality and the poor have become more primitive."[14] Besides accurately forecasting the current vogue for parabiosis, cryogenics, and the Singularity among the would-be Eternals of Silicon Valley—perhaps with Huxley's *Many a Summer Dies the Swan* in mind—Boorman's focus on class conflict was continuous with earlier films such as *Leo the Lion.*

Yet Boorman tells a different tale regarding the genesis and development of *Zardoz* in an interview he gave concurrently with the film's release. Boorman's original story was set a few years in the future and focused on a professor searching for a student among the communes and intentional communities of Northern California. In researching the film, Boorman "went up to Northern California and visited a number of communes to see what this kind of life was like, and I found it mostly rather sterile." He does not elaborate on the character of this "sterility"—a term not often associated with the back-to-the-land movement—beyond observing of these arrangements that "where there was a basic need, some practical sharing, it worked, but the communes based on ideology collapsed at the slightest pressure."[15] It was from this experience that *Zardoz's* techno-utopian vision of the Vortex and its Eternals emerged: "I became increasingly intrigued about where the commune idea might lead, supposing that our society collapsed, and the communes were all that survived. Then I thought of there being an elite of privileged people who would have the technology to survive, using a kind of Earth Spaceship that would be regenerative and protected from the outside world."[16]

Boorman's evocation of Buckminster Fuller's Spaceship Earth—a technological metaphor that drew on the space program, a technocratic version of environmentalism as resource management, and Fuller's own cybernetic model of social organization—implies that the sterility resided in those countercultural segments out of which our own Silicon Valley emerged. This technocentric strain of counterculture—dubbed "the California Ideology"[17] by critics Richard Barbrook, Andy Cameron, and Fred Turner— is most often linked with Steward Brand and his Whole Earth Catalog, a kind of analog internet prototype, and at least some of the era's intentional communities. As Turner documents, this same hippie modernism—broadly libertarian in ethos and enamored of an alternative technology that was still decidedly high tech—transmogrified into yet another version of entrepreneurial individualism during the first wave of the dot-com boom in the Nineties. But, in keeping with its history, this entrepreneurial individualism maintained its alternative lifestyle costume, from high-end organic food to domesticated psychedelic drug use, evacuated of any substantively radical social content, as critical Aquarians like Boorman foresaw early on. We might even discern in the high-tech survivalist fantasies of present-day techno-oligarchs Thiel, Musk, and their SV fellow travelers an updated version of Boorman's elite techno-communes.

Yet those same critics who trace the lines of continuity between this segment of the counterculture and our post-Keynesian capitalist arrangement and ideology—alternately dubbed "neoliberalism," "capitalist realism," and "the new spirit of capitalism"—too often mistake one tendency of the counterculture for the counterculture as such: a common error in discussions of a monolithic Sixties. Perhaps the sterile first-world technocracy that Boorman saw in the Northern California communes of the time is part of what poet-critic Stephen Paul Miller sees as the broad turn toward disciplinary self-surveillance in the United States during the Seventies, which begins with "incorporating Sixties mores" while "disavowing the subversive content of those mores."[18] Miller offers us a very Seventies paranoid-conspiratorial account of the transition from utopian aspiration to neoliberalism's cynical reason, whereby Watergate-era state surveillance and the resistance to such surveillance on the part of the new left and counterculture alike gives way to self-surveillance and the widespread internalization of state and capitalist imperatives, expanded to encompass formerly marginalized lifestyles and identities in commodified form.

Miller, in his early account of the neoliberal (and postmodern) turn, does not recognize how these tendencies were present in some segments of a variegated counterculture from the start, nor how what critic Matt Tierney calls the "long Seventies" also witnessed the emergence of a Luddite or neo-Luddite constellation of "poets, activists, and thinkers, each of whom applies literature to the task of dismantling the technocentric world."[19] Tierney focuses on the work of Audre Lorde, Ursula Le Guin, Thomas Pynchon, Edouard Glissant, and W.S. Merwin, among others. While Tierney's project is in many ways congruent with my own—*Zardoz* is an exemplary work of Seventies-era neo-Luddism—what I call "critical Aquarianism" was both more expansive in its concerns and, often, more opposed to what its proponents saw as poisonous technological systems. Tierney sometimes attempts to salvage the orthodox Marxist dream of liberated forces of production or high technology in the form of cyberculture, which he contrasts with a wholly negative technocentric and ecocidal "cosmopolitics." The problem is not "technology" but the instrumentalization of human life."[20]

Yet the radicalism of so many Critical Aquarians resides in their rejection of this easy distinction between neutral instrument use and the instrument users' own instrumentalization by the various sociotechnological systems that organize modern life, from the petroleum-automobile complex to an iatrogenic medical-industrial complex or a (then-nascent) digital technosphere. Despite the military origins of our internet—developed for domestic counterinsurgency, as detailed by Yasha Levine[21]—its first countercultural enthusiasts saw in its decentralized architecture a utopian alternative technology; this line of thinking—whereby the seemingly decentralized network is contrasted with bad because centralized, industrial technologies—was prevalent during the Nineties-era dot-com wave, with its attendant techno-utopianism. Yet it was Langdon Winner—a guiding light of Tierney's Seventies neo-Luddism—who disputed, at great length, those theories that equate industrial technology with centralization as such. For Winner, the ideological fantasy of "autonomous technology" and autonomous technological development—an end-in-itself that curiously overlaps with the capitalist growth imperative—drives our destructive "technological politics." Rather than tools or technologies serving human needs and ends, these technological politics entail a process of "reverse adaptation" under which human needs and ends are reshaped in accordance with socio-technological systems—centralized and decentralized alike.[22]

Boorman anatomizes these same cybercultural illusions of a participatory, because decentralized, technology in the form of the Tabernacle. The Eternals' Vortex is managed by an artificial super-intelligence, known as the Tabernacle, that is only apparently immaterial but—as Zed learns—located in a crystal communing with other crystals: a network of individualized crystal rings attached to each Eternal, with which each Eternal communicates with both Tabernacle, fellow Eternals, and the Vortex as a whole. The Eternals ostensibly constitute the Vortex and the Tabernacle— used interchangeably in Boorman's novelization of the film—which allows them to reach various levels of collective consciousness and think together as one collective mind. Here is what at first appears a very Aquarian or New Age vision of communion—by way of crystals even!

Yet this thinking together almost always revolves around punishing those Eternals who violate the norms of the techno-commune by "aging" them. Once aged, these senile and abject dissidents and malefactors are designated "renegades" and segregated together as such. Like the Sibyl of Cumae, they can grow old, but they cannot die. But what they want most of all is to die, which is why they see in Zed the promise of liberation. The widespread discontent within the Vortex, among both renegades and those "Apathetics" who have lost the will to live, undercuts the claim to a collective consciousness facilitated by virtual technology that is first promulgated by Consuella, the most ardent adherent of the Vortex before she turns against it, ostensibly for Zed. As Avalow (Sally Anne Newton), the "priestess" type gifted with foresight, declares in response to Zed's appearance in the Vortex: "How did we conjure up a monster in our midst, and why? This is the question we must answer."[23] Zed later learns that the Vortex was designed—in a moment of ecological catastrophe—as an "ark" to "settle somewhere to restart the Earth," while the "reviving system which brought them back to life here was for spaceflight. If these ships were travelling light-years," they needed this "eternalizing machinery." Finally, "the mediation, the communal mind" was devised "to keep them spiritually strong and bound together.[24]

Boorman, here, offers us a perfect parable of Winner's "reverse adaptation," even as he holds the mirror to hippie modernists such as Stewart Brand. The Vortex is a false utopia animated by a false communion built on exclusion, extraction, and the fantasy of repurposing megatechnical systems against these systems' designs and architectures. Yet, rather than discounting the utopian impulse or communion as such, *Zardoz* depicts a model of communion that arises in opposition to "teletechnological ideals of global togetherness,"[25] such as Fuller's Spaceship Earth. Communion, achieved through flesh-and-blood struggle, forges solidarity and a new collective subject out of disparate, or even opposed, groups such as colonized Brutals and the various discontented segments of their Eternal colonizers.

The preexisting rot within the Vortex, prior to Zed's final, Vortex-dissolving confrontation with the Tabernacle, shows us that our Artificial Intelligence, rather than a projection of the Eternals' collective will, is a system of command that has successfully co-opted the Eternals' individual and collective agencies in a proleptic vision of our own internet. This last point is made explicit when Zed confronts and kills the still-living, and now apathetic architect of the Tabernacle, programmed so that its Eternal wards will forget the circumstances and aims of its design and construction. The gift of death is an expansive act of neo-Luddite dismantling, but one that is very much tied to a set of counter-modernist norms regarding human flourishing: such flourishing starts with an embrace of our mortality and natality, our embodiment and animality, of our fragility and the interdependence that follows from this. These are the broad lines that define Critical Aquarianism against a narrow neo-Malthusian politics of scarcity or "lifeboat ethics," on the one hand, and a techno-cornucopian modernist Marxism on the other.

III

ZARDOZ, CRITICAL AQUARIANISM, AND THE MALTHUSIAN MOMENT

Justin Sully, in an essay entitled "On the Cultural Projection of the Popular Crisis: The Case of *The Omega Man*," sees in the notably dystopian "outpouring" of popular science fiction films of the early-to-middle 1970s a "concentrated cultural expression of popular anxieties about population."[26] While Sully focuses on Boris Sagal's *The Omega Man* (1971), he names Boorman's *Zardoz* alongside *Soylent Green* (1973), *ZPG: Zero Population Growth* (1972), and *Logan's Run* (1976) as "even more explicit examples of demographic fantasy" (Sully 100). *Zardoz*—the plot of which centers around a managed neo-Malthusian dystopia complete with a giant stone head preaching population control to his exterminator acolytes in the form of "hygienic" murder ("The gun is good! The penis is evil")—is also a cinematic response to Sixties- and Seventies-era concerns over environmental degradation and overpopulation. Even as many of the films Sully mentions reproduce racially coded neo-Malthusian fears of "overpopulation," especially in the underdeveloped world, equating environmental deterioration with population pressure in the process, *Zardoz* notably offers a critical depiction of "population control" as ruling class ruse. Boorman, for example, dramatizes the need for self-limitation in the overdeveloped capitalist world, in recognition of an ecological crisis that has little to do with overpopulation as such, especially among the "wretched of the earth."

Zardoz offers us one critical and imaginative engagement with both neo-Malthusianism and the nascent environmental movement, distinct concerns with respectively distinct political programs that were too often identified with each other at the time due to the work of biologist Paul Ehrlich, whose bestselling *The Population Bomb* (1968) rang the alarm over human population growth, especially in the developing world. Ehrlich simplistically offered population growth outstripping scarce resources as the great driver of poverty, famine, and war, updating Thomas Malthus's 1798 *Essay on Population*—in which Malthus argued, in response to prevailing conditions in 1790s England, that while food supplies increase arithmetically, human population increases geometrically—for the industrial and globalized late twentieth century. Of course, Malthus's aims were explicitly political and conservative in character, as he argued for the inescapability of poverty against both ameliorative Poor Laws and the more utopian schemes for generalized human equality promoted by 1790s-era perfectibilists such as Godwin and Condorcet. Ehrlich's neo-Malthusian polemic was hardly conservative in this way, as he married his fear of overpopulation to a prescient concern with the environmental degradation produced by "advanced" production (and consumption) technologies and techniques in ways that resonated with the work of pioneering environmentalists such as Aldo Leopold and Rachel Carson.

Ehrlich—and the entire population control movement during this period—exhibited an ideological Janus face. Ehrlich and his fellow Zero Population Growth (ZPG) activists advocated expansive access to birth control, abortion, and expanded freedoms for women outside the traditional maternal role; in fact, radical feminists such as Lucinda Cisler and Shulamith Firestone initially worked together alongside ZPG in pursuit of these goals. As historian Thomas Robertson notes: "Because of the often bitter clashes between feminists and environmental Malthusians in the 1970s, many have forgotten that they were allies for much of the 1950s and 1960s."[27] It was for this reason that Ehrlich was such a hero to wide sections of the counterculture, as he argued for the rejection of restrictive sexual and gender norms in his response to Pope Paul VI's 1968 encyclical *Humanae Vitae*, in which the Pope reaffirmed the Catholic Church's total ban on birth control, declaring that reproduction should be left in God's (or nature's) hands. Ehrlich, in response, called for the conscious and rational regulation of human reproduction. Critics at the time noted the seeming inconsistency between Ehrlich's opposition to human technological interference in the natural world and his call for human technological maintenance of human reproduction and population.

What is telling for our purposes is Ehrlich's response to this apparent inconsistency: trust the experts. Population growth—and environmental crises—must be managed by demographers and scientific ecologists rather than the women who have children, for example. The problem here is not expertise or scientific knowledge as such, but the supremely ideological gesture whereby such knowledge is proffered as a neutral substitute for ethical reflection and political contention, especially with regard to issues such as family planning, that encompass fact and value. It was this brand of technocratic authoritarianism, which takes a more nakedly coercive and reactionary form in the work of fellow neo-Malthusian Garret Hardin, from which feminists and other representatives of the counterculture so violently broke in the Seventies. But perhaps it was the "hippie modernist" segment of the counterculture who gravitated toward Ehrlich's technocratic vision in the first place? The same sterile hippie modernists Boorman saw in at least some of the communes of Northern California? Stewart Brand saw in these communes a more resource-efficient form of social organization perfectly suited to a still-nascent decentralized computer network technology: the internet.[28] With the collapse of the Back to the Land Movement, Brand transferred his enthusiasm to small-scale cities, horizontal corporations, and space colonies (for which the communes offered a test run according to Brand). Or, as Boorman describes the origins of the Vortex in the novelization of his film:

> So it was an ark, set adrift to await the ebbing of the flood.
> It was planned to settle somewhere and restart the Earth,
> or if the waters never receded, to sail on forever, drifting
> helplessly, yet thriving within.[29]

Contrary to popular belief, many of the participants in these experiments shared the techno-modernist assumptions of the establishment they purported to reject, albeit in a superficially heterodox form. While this strand of the counterculture would go on to reshape the face of US culture and capitalism in the form of Silicon Valley and the digital internet complex that rose to prominence in the Nineties, we can nonetheless find genuinely radical challenges to the logic of capitalist modernity among other Critical Aquarian movements and thinkers; as David Cayley writes of Ivan Illich during the brief period when his ideas were prominent and popular: "This was also a period of what Illich called 'ethical awakening' when at least a potential majority recognized that the Western project of remaking the world had reached a crisis, and that a moment of decision was at hand." Illich, and other Critical Aquarian thinkers and artists such as Boorman, "spoke to this moment and outlined the marriage of playfulness, austerity, and sense of scale that he felt would be necessary to counteract the prevailing technomania and institutional hubris."[30]

And technomania—a figure that encompasses the global north's expropriation of wealth and resources in the service of an ecocidal mode of production and consumption—is the root of the problem rather than overpopulation, as Boorman dramatizes in his film. Techno-cornucopians today reduce "Malthusianism" to a primitivism, despite the fact that this model of biopolitical management is explicitly linked to specifically capitalist modes of growth and work discipline, beginning with Malthus, then accumulation, uneven ecological exchange, and a technocratic vision of resource management in its neo-Malthusian form. While Spaceship Earth represents the most benign face of this technocratic Malthusianism, Hardin's contemporaneous "lifeboat" ethic illuminates the neocolonial and often frankly eugenicist side of population politics that were, in part, the object of *Zardoz*'s critical satire. Hardin rejected Fuller's one-world metaphor of the spaceship as "suicidal"; he instead analogized environmental degradation and resource scarcity—incorrectly equated with overpopulation—to several lifeboats, in which already full and well-equipped boats were taking on too many of the wrong passengers. Hardin, in other words, advocated immigration restrictions, especially when it was people immigrating from the global south to the global north, despite the latter's extraction of key resources from the former while upholding the positive role of famine, war, and natural catastrophe in regulating the wretched of the earth against all relief efforts in a classically Malthusian fashion.[31]

One contender for a Critical Aquarian alternative to these frameworks is Lynn Margulis and James Lovelock's Gaia hypothesis, according to which the Earth is a self-regulating system and a living thing. Lovelock moved between Gaian science, which drew on the cybernetic models also beloved by Brand and the hippie modernists, and Gaian metaphor, rooted in its evocation of the ancient Greek Earth goddess, that imagines the biosphere as a unique super-organism. Despite Lovelock's late life turn to techno-utopianism, his early work, like that of Margulis's, was very much written against the mechanistic reductionism implicit in both the lifeboat and spaceship metaphors: "[Gaia] is an alternative to that pessimistic view which sees nature as a primitive force to be subdued and conquered. It is also an alternative to that equally depressing picture of our planet as a demented spaceship, travelling, driverless and purposeless, around an inner circle of the sun."[32]

Zardoz's Eternals—partly inspired by the budding technocrats Boorman saw in the communes of Northern California—invent a decidedly Malthusian religion to manage the Brutal population of an ecologically decimated Earth in the form of Zardoz commanding his Exterminator devotees to murder everyone they see while refraining from reproduction themselves. Zardoz is also an audio-animatronic god, a floating stone head under the operation of Frayn, the Eternals' dissident wizard figure, that dispenses the weaponry with which Zed and his murderous compatriots kill the Brutal masses, in keeping with these superhuman technocrats' Hardinesque program of population and resource management. The sadism that marks the Exterminator program, which includes non-reproductive sex in the form of rape (Fig 12), belies the Eternals' utilitarian rationale.

In scanning his memory, Eternals May and Consuella force him to relive his aggressions—a process that provokes remorse and empathy in Zed as he learns the truth behind Zardoz or the "jackanapes in god's clothing": "They would always live in the darkness of fear, ignorance, and exploitation. Furthermore, they had to worship and obey. If he abandoned them—without his guns, outnumbered by the Brutals as they were—they would all be wiped away in days. Worst of all, Zardoz had turned them against their own race. They were genocidal soldiers—killing their own stock, spilling their own people's blood in the name of a foreign and grotesque alien cause."[33]

Zed understands that he has always been a cop and a comprador, a native agent of foreign powers, though unbeknownst to himself because he is under the spell of a techno-religious cargo cult. Zed's development in this way echoes the trajectory of certain "third world" intellectuals, educated under their respective colonial regimes, during the era of decolonization. This realization allows Zed to assume his mission: the destruction of the Vortex, the Tabernacle, and the Eternals as eternal. This reading, however, is complicated by the revelation that Zed himself was engineered by Frayn and other dissident Eternals seeking the "gift of death" for both themselves and their immortal social order.

In a moment marked by growing ecological awareness and third-world liberation movements brought home to the capitalist core by the Vietnam War, many saw in the neo-Malthusian turn a revanchist response to the insurgent peoples of the decolonizing world, made explicit in the writing of Hardin and those Zero Population Growth advocates who reserved their coercive population control measures for the peoples of the global south. These concerns inspired Boorman, who developed the idea for the film as a means of dramatizing a global situation in which "we, the people of the developed world are extending our lifespan through advances in medicine, while the majority of the world is getting poorer and more abject."[34]

Hence, Zed learns that the Brutal majority is maintained by the Immortal elite as human stock for both the maintenance of the Vortex, the Immortals' technologically advanced fusion of commune and ark, and their abortive program of space colonization. Zed also discovers that the sudden shift in Zardoz's commands—from extermination to enslavement of Brutals, specifically to grow wheat—was driven by the nutritional needs of the Apathetics, those semi-catatonic Immortals whose population increases every year according to Friend. Here, we see how the lives of some "surplus" populations—in this case the Apathetics of Boorman's global north proxy—are more valuable than others, such as those Brutals indentured for the sake of the Vortex's elite catatonics: a biopolitics underwritten by global class inequities, in other words. The film in these ways echoes then-contemporary left critics of the overpopulation panic, such as Barry Commoner, who, in his extended debate with Ehrlich, made the point that "productive technologies with intense impacts on the environment have displaced less destructive ones. The environmental crisis is the inevitable result of this counterecological pattern of growth."[35] It is a resource-intensive and toxic technosphere coupled with first-world consumption patterns—rather than a global population number that ignores such production-consumption and its locations— that are at the heart of the problem. Planetary and biophysical boundaries to human development must be acknowledged (and were acknowledged in the more sophisticated analyses of ecological economists of the time), even as such development cannot be completely separated from the population question, as historian Derek S. Hoff quipped of the Ehrlich-Commoner debate: "Clearly, a global population of five hundred million, assuming current technologies, would leave a significantly reduced ecological footprint. Conversely, the planet might happily sustain many more billions if everyone lived like the Amish. Assessing the harmful effects of population growth and harmful technology are both important."[36]

While the affluence and high technology of the Eternals, dependent upon a genocidally extractive relationship with the Outlands, offers us a cinematic emblem for uneven ecological exchange between developed and developing worlds, the violent primitivism of the Exterminators—yet another example of these same would-be wizards' high-tech social control—is no alternative.

Boorman dramatizes Malthusianism as the flip side of its techno-cornucopian antagonist. Malthusian scarcity flows from the mismatch between ostensibly limitless human desires, which emerge from a fallen human nature, and the necessarily limited world of which we can never get enough—whether in the form of food, other resources, and ultimately time—to satisfy ourselves. But this mismatch and scarcity function as a spur to economic growth and development for Malthus and his technocratic heirs, as contemporary degrowth economist Giorgos Kallis notes: "the premise of unlimited human wants and of a natural and universal scarcity; the insistence on industry and growth as a response to scarcity" represents a "defense of inequality on the basis that it fosters industry."[37] The ideological specter of scarcity has been mobilized against redistributive measures from the eighteenth-century English Poor Laws to the international aid decried by Garrett Hardin, and always to "safeguard" economic growth and technological development—at least among the Eternals within the Vortex. An irony here is that even as present-day techno-futurists and transhumanists of the right and left use *Malthusian* as an epithet for anyone who suggests a fundamentally different eco-social order, they share Malthus's vision of an insatiable human nature, although without Malthus's negative gloss or any explicit invocation of human nature. Theirs is a post-human Prometheanism clothed in radical constructionist drag: we are desiring machines or cyborgs.

The Eternals are play utopians, whose utopia is built upon unseen human and ecological devastation. The Eternals are, for this reason, a pitch-perfect figure for today's transhumanists, for today's accelerationists, for today's *Star Trek* socialists. We can certainly draw a line from the hippie modernists and technocratic managers of the Zardozian moment to these people: their children.

What is finally notable about Boorman's fable in this regard is that these same Eternals, in satisfying (or supplanting) their every want and desire through technological magic, want nothing so much as to die.

IV

THE GIFT OF DEATH, ZED, AND UTOPIA LIMITED

It is during Zed's period of servitude under Friend that he is introduced to the Apathetics. The Apathetics represent that growing contingent of Eternals who have lapsed into a semi-catatonic state. Upon first encountering these Apathetics, Friend encourages his brutal pet Zed to molest one of the catatonic women, but she is completely unresponsive to Zed's assaults, deflating Connery's barbarian machismo (Fig. 13). These same

Apathetics exert a vampiric power over Zed, sapping his energy and nearly overwhelming him later in the narrative, even as the Vortex implodes. Friend outlines the situation: "Didn't Zardoz tell you about the Apathetics? No? It's a disease, and it's slowly creeping all through the Vortexes. That's why Zardoz made you grow crops—to feed these people. We can't support them anymore. Apathetic or Renegade—take your choice."[38]

This growing "apathy" within the Vortex necessitates the shift from a genocidally Malthusian mode of surplus population management in the Outlands to exploitation and resource extraction. Suddenly, the Eternals have their own sort of overpopulation problem, one that requires the same sort of Exterminator used by our immortal overlords for the purpose of Brutal population control. We later learn that Zed was engineered by a cabal of dissident or Renegade Eternals, including Frayn and Friend, to destroy both the Tabernacle and the Vortex, bringing the "gift of death" to the Eternals. The Apathetics link the political ecology of resource management, population control, and uneven ecological exchange with qualitative concerns and questions regarding what makes for a meaningful human life, highlighting the role of finitude and fragility in human flourishing.

Finitude and limitation—to be distinguished from the artificial scarcities of market society—are the precondition for any substantive human freedom or meaning-making enterprise; as philosopher Martin Hägglund pithily notes: "If what happens *matters* and our actions have *consequences*, it is because they are irreversible and cannot be undone. If they could be undone, what we say and do would not have the significance it does. The sense that something matters emerges from a secular faith, which contains the commitment to a finite and fragile form of life."[39]

Hägglund draws on a long philosophical tradition that argues for the centrality of transience and mortality in thinking through our creaturely condition, in outlining his "secular faith" model. Finitude encompasses more than the fact of our inevitable expiration; we are thrown into a world we do not choose, with limited time as beings who die. It is exactly these limits—to choose to do this rather than that, with the limited time that you have, to commit to this person or project, knowing that such commitments might fail, bringing with that failure an irretrievable loss of your limited time—that lend our lives weight or significance. It is only against these necessary limit conditions that human freedom is any way coherent, keeping with a certain strand of German Idealism, exemplified by Hegel, that underlines exactly this dialectic of freedom and necessity. An earlier Critical Aquarian thinker— whose work we will examine in some detail below—makes a similar point regarding the relationship between death and individuality: "The precious ontological uniqueness which the human individual claims is conferred on him not by possession of an immortal soul but a mortal body. Without death, Hegel argues, we are reduced to the status of mere modes in the one infinite and eternal substance of Spinoza."[40]

While we often associate this mode of thinking with existentialism and the ever-controversial work of Martin Heidegger—Hägglund's *This Life* arguably represents a fusion of Hegelian Marxism and Heidegger's philosophy of finitude, at least in part—it was during the Critical Aquarian moment that death, that most significant of limits, entered popular consciousness in exactly those "advanced" industrial capitalist societies, such as the United States, defined by a widespread "denial of death." *The Denial of Death* is the title of cultural anthropologist Ernest Becker's 1973 *cri di coeur*, which won the Pulitzer Prize in 1974 after Becker's own ironically sudden death from cancer; Becker's book, and the work of psychologist Elizabeth Kubler-Ross, promoted a new openness to death and grieving.

The proximate source of this tendency at the time, regarding human finitude, was the work of radical social critic and unlikely countercultural prophet Norman O. Brown, beginning with his visionary *Life Against Death* (1959), then elaborated and refined in poetic and aphoristic form during the later Sixties and early Seventies in his *Love's Body* (1966) and *Closing Time* (1973). Brown describes his first great work as "The Psychoanalytic Meaning of History" in the subtitle: a grandiloquent precis that still understates the speculative ambition of an argument seeking to revise and combine elements of Freudian psychoanalysis with the Hegelian philosophy of history, Christian theology, phenomenology, and literary hermeneutics. Brown transforms the most pessimistic, and theoretically inconsistent, component of Freud's work— his late and various theorizations of a death drive as the motive force, alongside Eros, impelling the human project—into the counterintuitive foundation for his own utopian hopes.

Late in his life, Freud revised his earlier theory of libido, or a sexual impulse in excess of any instinct of self-preservation, as the driving force behind human psychic life, in positing a separate death drive in a series of texts written after the First World War. He initially saw this drive at work in the compulsion to repeat that he observed in children, including his nephew, and various neurotic patients. According to Freud, this unconscious drive seeks a return to an earlier and inactive organic or even pre-organic state free from all tension and akin to homeostasis; it should be noted that Freud earlier attributed this drive toward what he identifies as nirvana with the libido or Eros, but in the course of developing his theory of Thanatos, we see some slippage between these terms, even as he sketches a dualistic metapsychology whereby humans are caught between an urge toward that tensionless inorganic state—or Thanatos—and Eros, the drive into greater unities.

Freud again reverses himself in positing a primary masochism in early childhood—that death drive again—that is later displaced and projected outward in the form of sadism and the human proclivity toward violence. These inconsistencies are key to Brown's own creative reinterpretation, exemplified in this bravura riff on nirvana, repression, history, and repression as history that deserves quotation in full:

The reunification of Life and Death—accepting for a moment Freud's equation of Death and Nirvana—can be envisioned only at the end of the historical process. Freud's pessimism, his preference for dualism rather than dialectics, and his failure to develop an eschatology are all of a piece. To see how man separated from nature, and separated out the instincts, is to see history as neurosis; and also to see history, as neurosis, pressing restlessly and unconsciously toward the abolition of history and the attainment of a state of rest which is also a reunification with nature. It comes to the same thing to say that the consequence of the disruption of the unity of Life and Death in man is to make man the historical animal. For the restless pleasure-principle—which is the morbid manifestation of the Nirvana principle—is what makes man Faustian, and Faustian man is history-making man. If repression were overcome, the restless career of Faustian man would come to an end, because he would be satisfied.[41]

For Brown, it is repression that severs life from death drive, with the resultant externalization of these impulses as a will to power and an urge to destroy, subjugate, and transform other human beings and the natural world, i.e., history. As Brown does not hide the ecstatically religious and romantic aims that guide his project—from the reunification with an idyllic natural world from which we have expelled ourselves to a polymorphously perverse resurrection of the body in the key of William Blake—it is no wonder that his work was such a touchstone for the Sixties counterculture. Brown nonetheless begins his analysis in tragic recognition of humankind's centaur condition, caught between our first (animal, fragile, finite) nature and a second one encompassing language, culture, and the repression they require, so often marshalled in denial of that first nature and our place within it. Freud confuses life and death drives, according to Brown, because they are one and the same. It is only the process of repression that divides them, and in the case of Thanatos, this repression and displacement is projected outward, most explicitly in the form of the murderous violence dramatized in *Zardoz*'s Exterminators and the techno-modernist population management program they unknowingly enforce.

Keeping Marcuse's useful distinction between necessary and surplus repression in mind here: while Brown's call for a completely non-repressed human life in some ways overlaps with the consumerist fantasy of limitless desire, his vision of the "resurrected body" presents the embrace of certain limits as the beginning of liberation. Death must be unrepressed alongside the Eros with which Thanatos is entwined, according to Brown, who contends that human renewal requires the embrace of embodied life and finitude, most of all. Here are synecdoches for a creaturely condition that includes the contingency, natality, and animality that form a bridge with non-human nature. And this shift in perspective informed both Critical Aquarianism and the Zardozian counterpoint to the neo-Malthusianism I have mapped in this essay: "The death instinct is reconciled with the life instinct only in a life which is not repressed, which leaves no 'unlived lines' in the human body, the death instinct then being affirmed in a body which is willing to die."[42]

To truly love life: we must accept death. To build a better life, individually and in common: we must accept death. And to deny death leads to a culture of death, as we project death outward onto others and the earth in attempting to avoid and repress our own finitude.

Brown draws utopian conclusions—an unrepressed bodily life—from the acceptance of limits or the one great limit; many of his interlocutors and heirs rejected these conclusions even as they adopted his concerns and certain elements of his argument. Becker, for example, concludes his *Denial of Death* by accepting Brown's call to embrace death as inextricable from life and meaning, which requires a kind of heroism, while rejecting Brown's call to jettison repression, as he writes, invoking the more orthodox Freudian Phillip Rieff, "in order to have a truly human existence there must be limits. Culture is a compromise with life that makes human culture possible."[43]

Christopher Lasch similarly eschews Brown's rejection of repression *tout court*, even as Lasch identifies himself as a Critical Aquarian fellow traveler in his embrace of limits and through his critique of a later-Seventies culture of narcissism, looking forward to the Reagan era and its aftermaths. Lasch, in works such as *The Culture of Narcissism* and *The Minimal Self*, connects the technological mediation of everyday life with a mass retreat into a shallow and deracinated selfhood. Lasch in this way looks forward to our own age of the selfie as he builds on Hannah Arendt's definition of "modern world alienation": "a twofold flight from the earth into the universe and from the world into the self."[44] As the cultural upheaval of the Sixties curdled into various forms of co-optation, commodification, and restoration during the Seventies, this process intensified, with some segments of the counterculture lending a hand, as we have seen. The neo-Luddites and dissident psychoanalytic social critics as well as radical ecologists and remnant romantics whom I have grouped under the Critical Aquarian umbrella charted this process in their diagnoses of autonomous technology, iatrogenesis, and a culture of narcissism. Or they tracked such transformationas in the visionary form of *Zardoz's* phantasmagoria of ideas.

Brown's vision of life and death reconciled after repression—what he calls the "resurrection of the body" in a profane reconstitution of the Christian myth—in the manner of homeostasis also evokes the convivial technologies of Illich or the steady state economy envisaged by ecological economists Herman Daly or Nicholas Georgescu-Roegen.

These ecological economists advocated a sustainable metabolic relationship between human beings and a natural world that incorporated entropy rather than increasing it through cancerous patterns of industrial growth driven by exchange-value rather than the needs of creaturely life. We see the same program articulated by the degrowth movement today. Brown's flights of speculation are useful prods toward thinking, and even his solutions, too often dismissed as Sixties era sexual mysticism, offer suggestive ways of tracing relations between the human unconscious and the natural world, for example, or industrial capitalism and psychopathology, especially if we historicize his ideas. These ideas—so alien to twenty-first century sensibilities marked by a popular technophilia, for which even death is amenable to some technical solution, and a radical constructionism, whereby once-foundational terms such as "nature" and "the unconscious" are just so many discursive constructs—certainly informed the zeitgeist out of which *Zardoz* came. Perhaps this is why this work appears so peculiar to us. Brown's effort to synthesize Freud's account of the repetition compulsion with the Hegelian theory of history was most of all an indictment aimed at the stagist ideologies of progress and developmentalism that, Cold War aside, united the Cold War's antagonists.

Brown recasts this neurotically ineffectual drive to recapture the past as the psychotically destructive drive to build a bigger, better, death-free future in the Faustian pattern. We can see in Brown's account a counter-myth of industrial modernity: growth for growth's sake or the valorization of capitalist exchange-value as an end-in-itself, or human beings maladapting themselves to the complex technological systems ostensibly built to serve those human beings. Brown sees the neurotic's repetition compulsion behind the constant churn of techno-capitalist "innovation," whereby endless novelty masks the eternal recurrence of the same, ever worsening with each reiteration, like the ceaselessly regrown bodies of Boorman's Eternals who grow increasingly defective as a result.

With some degree of elective affinity, Illich also describes a pattern of "counterproductivity which is now surfacing in all major industrial sectors. Like time-consuming acceleration, stupefying education, self-destructive military defense, disorienting information or unsettling housing projects, pathogenic medicine is the result of industrial overproduction that paralyzes autonomous action."[45] Psychopathological symptoms indeed: Illich was a heterodox religious thinker like Brown, albeit in a different mold. Illich and Brown nonetheless concur in their estimations of a counterproductive, self-defeating and increasingly genocidal industrial system that, in fetishizing health—understood as the quantitative maintenance of bare life without any regard for qualitative concerns and ends—and denying finitude leads to the displaced reign of the death instinct.

(There is no greater image of bare life, arranged according to the planner's utilitarian calculus, and living death than *Zardoz's* Apathetics; there is no greater image of the refusal of this regime than *Zardoz's* Renegades. Both groups beg for death to lend their limitless lives' meaning, at least retroactively.)

What we see in the neo-Malthusian drive toward population management or the quantitative management of populations as resources—sorting populations into "good" and "bad," "healthy" or "diseased," murdering some, or at least letting them die to efficiently optimize "life" and "health" and "progress" for the greatest number, in the present or over the long term—is the death drive, repressed or distorted because it is cleaved from life and Eros. Qualitatively distinct lives with their distinctive projects are rendered interchangeable integers when reduced to population units—a collection of statistical probabilities—to be maximized, minimized, optimized, but always manipulated: exactly bare life (or living death). As Michel Foucault, an unlikely Critical Aquarian fellow traveler, argued, there is a biopolitical core—a technocratic will-to-power—at the heart of the various utilitarianisms that mark the intellectual superstructures of the industrial capitalist moment—from Bentham, Malthus, and the neo-Malthusian population managers of the 1970s to their putative "opponents" today, such as those "long-termists" focused on maximizing long-term human survival and supremacy by any means necessary. So much of the Critical Aquarian vision, both theoretical and artistic, was counterposed against "the entropy machine," after Thomas Pynchon[46]: here was an alternative discourse of limits as the precondition for good living.

And while the many critics of neo-Malthusianism underlined its racist and neocolonial dimensions vis-a-vis the developing world—First World Immortals regulating the lives and deaths of the brutal masses beyond the Vortex—the Critical Aquarian perspective offers a useful complement to this analysis in its focus on the psychopathologies of the core exemplified by its Promethean masters' simultaneous drive for surplus extraction and biopolitical control. Finally, the Zardozian insistence on limits in a qualitative sense includes self-limitation, individual and collective, as Kallis underlines in exploring the difference between the Ancients and the Moderns regarding these matters: "the Greeks did not think of self-limitation as suffering. They saw limitation as normal (and suffering as a part of life). It is obvious that we have to master and craft our instincts; this is the price of civilization. The problem with us moderns is not that we have suppressed the death instinct, but by refusing death, we are only able to react to death through violence: we attempt to overcome it by subduing nature or by shifting death onto others. Accepting death and accepting their violent instincts, Greeks tried to master their instincts."[47]

Zed can do neither, initially. He was conceived as a Frankenstein's monster, according to Boorman, designed by Frayn and a cabal of dissident Eternals specifically to undo them and the Vortex itself. As Boorman explains: "They needed him at that point. And it refers back to Arthur Frayn's conjuring tricks, as well as to the Frankenstein legend—the way he has produced and invented this creature, and the way he comes into society and horrifies them."[48] While Frankenstein's creature is one prototype for this character, another even more significant referent would be male lead Connery's signature role: James Bond. Zed was one of the first major roles Connery took—incredibly—after departing the James Bond franchise (alongside *The Offence*). Zed's trajectory is arguably a sci-fi/primitive pastiche of the spy franchise: Zed, like Bond, murders and rapes with a license to do so, so to speak, provided by his false god, all in the service of an imperial agenda of which Zed is unaware until he discovers the man behind the mask or, in this instance, inside that flying stone head. Speaking of *Frankenstein*— Mary Shelley's "Modern Prometheus"—we can discern in Zed, the god-killer who gives the gift of death (and limits) to his Eternal overlords, a revisionist version of the mythical thief of fire. Our professional killer turns on his makers, by design, although, as Zed says to Frayn during the Vortex's immolation: "I have looked into the face of the force that put the idea into your head. You are led and bred yourself."[49]

Perhaps the Frankensteinism is most evident in this final suggestion: Gaia still bats last. Zed is in many ways a parody of postwar machismo—as evinced in the series of ridiculous outfits Connery is made to wear over the course of the film (figure 14b)—despite contemporary critics of the film who saw in Zed a celebration of retrograde masculinity, like Marsha Kinder who situates Boorman in a tradition of "formidable misogynists" such as "Swift, Mailer, Burroughs, Jodorowsky, Kubrick, and Peckinpah."[50] For Kinder, the film's conclusion represents a valorization of the nuclear family. Zed, on the contrary, is a dead end, and insofar as the enigmatic conclusion to the film suggests an alternative to both Eternals and Exterminators, Promethean modernism and primitivist reaction, that alternative is offscreen, a point to which I will return in my conclusion.

These considerations are difficult for political modernists and Marxists alike, as they equate limits with the artificial scarcities of the market while refusing to engage with the qualitative question of what makes for human flourishing, partly due to the old Marxist ban on abstract utopian speculation. Yet the embrace of utopian speculation among certain Western Marxists too often represents the return of a transcendental religious urge in techno-utopian guise, as we can see in the work of Fredric Jameson, who grappled with *Zardoz* at the time and in terms that look forward to his later, better-known work on utopia and postmodernism.

V

JAMESON'S ENGAGEMENT, THE LIMITS OF MODERNIST MARXISM, AND THE ZARDOZIAN MOMENT

Western Marxist literary critic and theorist Fredric Jameson offers us one of the few contemporaneous academic engagements with *Zardoz* in an essay entitled "History and the Death Wish: *Zardoz* as Open Form," published in the 1974 issue of cinema studies journal *Jump Cut*. The essay, written before the critic's better-known theorizations of the utopian impulse and the postmodern turn, prefigures this later work in its focus on *Zardoz*'s "open form" or the formal ambiguity that allows for the coexistence of "reactionary" and "progressive" elements in Boorman's film, or what Jameson will later dub the "dialectic of ideology and utopia."

Jameson—more dogmatically Marxist during this early, new-left affiliated phase of his intellectual development—disapproves of the film's ideological ambiguity. For Jameson, this ambiguity flows from a cinematic form that, in its visual and narrative surfeit, allows multiple and contradictory readings; the critic likens this form to "fable." While Jameson's new-left commitments provide a useful optic for reading Boorman's film, in part, his modernist Marxism also hinders his grasp of Boorman's Critical Aquarian vision. There are, for example, continuities between what Jameson sees as the film's ideological antinomies: the indictment of a capitalist US and its exploitative relationship with the developing world, and its ostensibly anti-utopian satire rooted in a particular model of human nature.

Jameson begins his analysis of the film by reading its initial depiction of the giant stone head, the false god used by the Eternals to subjugate the Brutal majority, as Boorman's "redramatization" of "an idea of religion essentially developed by Enlightenment thinkers: namely, that all religious belief is a superstitious mystification perpetuated by a cruel and repressive apparatus of priests and oppressors."[51] It is, of course, Zed's suspicion regarding his idol's falsity that leads to his sneaking himself into the head, buried in the Exterminators' regular tribute of grain, after which he "kills" Frayn and crash lands in the Vortex.

Zed's skepticism toward Zardoz inaugurates our exterminator's disillusionment, as he uncovers the manipulative "priestcraft" of the Eternals behind both his false god and the reconstituted Bronze Age world of the Outlands, in line with Jameson's invocation of the anti-clerical Enlightenment. Zed also learns that he was engineered by a few of these same puppet masters—through the seemingly serendipitous discovery of Baum's *Wizard Of Oz* during one of the Exterminators' raids. This discovery awakens the still-dormant capacities baked into our savage messiah by Frayn to accomplish Frayn's purposes: to destroy the Vortex and bring its ennui-stricken Eternals "the gift of death." To focus on Boorman's critique of religion in Jameson's Enlightenment terms too narrowly abstracts one very partial point from a more complicated story. As much as that old time religion, *Zardoz* also exposes the

Eternals' secular hypermodernist faith in technological salvation (and biopolitical population management) as yet another, very dangerous, religious idol. And this double movement, against religious atavism and transhumanist delusion, accords with Boorman's own claims regarding his work, from *Zardoz* to *Excalibur* and *The Emerald Forest* (and beyond). In the mold of both the first generation romantics and his Critical Aquarian contemporaries, Boorman's work marries the critical interrogation of religion as "priestcraft," in Jameson's sense, with an appreciation of "this other power, which is called magic, but which could be called imagination or compassion."[52] As Tierney argues in regard to Jameson's influential Seventies-era readings of fellow Critical Aquarian Ursula Le Guin, it is exactly the qualitative, or even romantic, dimensions of this work—and its relation to collective imagination, ethos, and alternative modes of communion—that elude Jameson's Marxist optic.

We can observe this admixture of insight and myopia in Jameson's dueling accounts of the Vortex. Jameson sees that "we Americans are ourselves the Vortex's Eternals, freed by the service economy from the drudgery of real labor and sheltered cosmetically from any real experience of death." But these "privileges" depend on "the violence of our mercenaries and the power of superstition and enforced ignorance" in extracting "the necessary riches from servile and miserable populations abroad. At length, even to ourselves, capitalism comes to seem a criminal attempt to tamper with the laws of nature (e.g., in terms of the film, to live forever)."[53]

Zardoz is very much a product of a post-Vietnam moment that witnessed dissident Western intellectuals and artists grappling with the Western colonial legacy and the extent to which the "first" world's overdevelopment required the underdevelopment of the "third" world. Boorman's fable—in linking the techno-magic of his Eternals to the exterminationist management of the Brutal majority, in addition to the Outlands' environmental devastation ("to tamper with the laws of nature" in other words)—points to contemporaneous theories of underdevelopment. The film and fable in this way portend later models of uneven ecological exchange, whereby our megamachines, necessarily confined to the few, require exploitation, despoliation, and entropy elsewhere, or in the formulation of Alf Hornborg: "The uneven accumulation of technological infrastructure signifies the confluence of thermodynamics and imperialism."[54]

Boorman arguably represents this post-Sixties convergence of third-world struggle and first-world dissidence in the tacit alliance between Zed the Barbarian—who brings death and, ultimately, the Brutal hordes to the Vortex's techno-oasis—and those Eternals who support (or even direct) his project to overturn the Tabernacle.

Yet, Jameson still cannot rid himself of his suspicions regarding the allegedly anti-utopian intentions that drive Boorman to judge "his Utopia from the outset," condemning "it to destruction. Thus, he deprives the film of some more interesting and ambiguous tension between the demands of life and the consequences of perfection."[55] Assimilating the representation (and ultimate destruction) of the Vortex to the post-Bolshevik and Cold War era ascendence of anti-totalitarian dystopian fiction, our critic concludes that this "is always a code word or disguise for refusing *socialism*. The anti-utopian strategy has as its function to eliminate from the outset the possibility of any speculation about human possibilities and the transformation of the social order."[56] While Jameson's conclusions might surprise some readers in the face of his alternative interpretation of the Vortex, this analysis also reveals exactly those modernist assumptions that underwrite Marxism, Soviet or Western, and the larger emancipatory project of which orthodox socialism is a part.

The young Jameson, in line with these traditions, can only equate the Vortex with "utopia"—or an emancipated social order—because he identifies "emancipation" with the fundamentally religious goal of human transcendence, albeit in the secular post-Enlightenment guise of "perfection." (This identification also accounts for his refusal to see that *Zardoz*'s pernicious false god refers as much to the post-Enlightenment dreams of Promethean mastery as to the old religion such dreams supposedly displaced.) This perfection primarily entails the conquest of our finite and fragile condition, often under the auspices of a perfected rationality, cleansed of affect and imagination and through which human beings will sever any trace of animality and ascend to god-hood. We see the first secular iterations of the modernist ideal-type in the work of such perfectibilists of the radical Enlightenment as Condorcet and Godwin, who dreamt of a progressive human developmental arc culminating in the millennial triumph of Reason and, with it, a perfectly rational, sexless, and immortal super-humanity. This vision persists in present-day techno-utopian visions of the Singularity, when human beings will merge with AI and become gods or Eternals.[57]

Since the early modern period, the ruling classes of Europe and its settler colonies have used such perfectibilism to mystify and rationalize the appropriation, exploitation, and colonization that forms the bedrock of capitalist modernity, as Jameson himself recognizes in his alternative reading. Yet this same fantasy of a perfected modernity—whereby an idealized material-technological development is equated with ethico-political progress and emancipation—infects modern utopian thinking and anticapitalism of all sorts, including the work of putative Western Marxist critics of modernity, enlightenment, and technology such as Theodor Adorno, whose own critical engagement with Aldous Huxley's *Brave New World*, "Aldous Huxley and Utopia," pervades Jameson's engagement with *London*.

While Adorno spends the first half of his own essay offering qualified praise for what he discerns as the novel's satirical vision of the totally administered world of bureaucratic capitalism and its culture industry, he criticizes Huxley for presenting yet another version of heroic individualism as alternative to the de-individualized techno-dystopia of the novel's One World State. In Adorno's words: "Unreflective individualism asserts itself as though the horror which transfixes the novel were not itself the monstrous offspring of individualist society."[58] The novel's would-be heroes—from Bernard Marx to Zed prototype John the Savage—are of course objects of derision for Huxley. Adorno, the would-be critic of orthodox Marxist "forces-of-productionism," reveals himself as, in fact, orthodox on these matters while anatomizing Huxley's "negative utopia," whose "inevitable character" arises "from projecting the limitations imposed by the relations of production (the enthronement of the productive apparatus for the sake of profit) as properties of the human and technical productive forces *per se.*"[59] In other words, the only limit is capitalism. This line of thinking points to the fundamentally religious character of utopia—which should not be described the same way that G-d must not be depicted lest we lapse into idolatry—for Adorno and intellectual protégé Jameson.

Boorman—like other Critical Aquarian thinkers and artists who had absorbed the lessons of the nascent ecological movement—seeks to distinguish the "utopian" impulse from Promethean fantasies of perfection in *Zardoz*. The film poses these questions, which are even more salient now in our era of catabolic capitalist ecological collapse: How to think utopia within limits? And how to distinguish the surplus limits imposed by an artificial and exploitative social arrangement from those necessary biophysical limits attendant upon our creaturely condition?

The parable of *Zardoz* concludes with Zed's reintroducing death into the Vortex, as its despairing Eternals beg for an ending at the hands of the Exterminators; but this orgy of death, which Jameson connects with a conservative vision of a fixed and violent human nature in the course of his anti-utopian reading, also serves as prelude to May, and her women followers, impregnated by Zed, departing the fallen Vortex to establish a new community that excludes Zed. The Exterminators' sanguinary alternative to the Eternals' bloodless simulacrum of life gives way to a third alternative after the dissolution of the Vortex.

Boorman's fable doesn't dispense with utopia so much as insist that our only feasible and substantive version of a liberated—

free and just—social order can only come by way of the natality, finitude, and embodiment we share. While our common creaturely condition offers a foundation for a more radical egalitarianism, the labor, life, and time we might win back from the impersonal imperatives of the market under another dispensation require the finitude that marks the condition we share with non-human creatures and their life-worlds.

Jameson himself would later discern in Soviet science fiction writer Andre Platonov's *Chevengur* exactly this sort of alternative utopia that he mistook for reactionary anti-utopianism in *Zardoz*. In a welcome departure from the Promethean and tacitly perfectibilist standpoint that suffuses too much of Jameson's writing on utopia, Jameson sees the lineaments of a "Heideggerian utopia"—a utopia with limits—in a reading of Platonov's novel *Chevengur* that resonates with Boorman's Critical Aquarianism. It is for this reason worth quoting at length:

> From [Platonov's] perspective Utopia is merely the material and political solution of collective life. It does not do away with the tensions and unresolvable contradictions inherent both in interpersonal relations and in bodily existence itself (among them those of sexuality), but rather exacerbates those and allows them free rein, by removing the artificial miseries of money and self-preservation. The Heideggerian perspective—which grants the achievement of the social Utopia the privilege of deconcealing Being itself—also opens up the experience of death that is at the heart of Being.[60]

Platonov's imaginary agrarian commune is one where the surplus repressions and injustices, the artificial scarcities, that flow from unjust social arrangements, such as class society, are abolished, allowing human beings to enjoy fully and, for the first time, the gift of life and the gift of death: one gift as we have seen. Aside from Heidegger's dark political associations, many of his most vocal critics focus on the extent to which the preferred Heideggerian vision of *Dasein*—human beings aligned with Being and Being-towards-Death through more rooted practices of thinking-working-dwelling—mystifies modern social relations by ignoring them, while tacitly positing a nostalgic vision of lord or peasant as ontological norm. While Jameson recognizes these mystifications under the present instance, he also sees that the substantive freedom and sense of purpose that comes out of necessity—which can only emerge after we remove "the artificial miseries of money and self-preservation"—exemplify a utopian impulse, albeit one that is very much at odds with most of the secular immortalisms that Jameson otherwise endorses (after Adorno and the broader Western Marxist tradition). Here is an example of "utopia, limited," in the formulation of literary critic Anahid Nersessian.[61]

I would also add—after our prior discussion of utopia's religious function in the Western Marxist tradition and Brown's Edenic endorsement of a new human life without repression or sublimation of any sort—that although we can and must eliminate the secondary alienation first defined by Karl Marx as the impersonal compulsion to alienate and sell our human powers and finite time in the marketplace under capitalism, we will never completely eliminate our primary alienation. Human beings are "natural aliens" in the memorable words of eco-phenomenologist Neil Evernden—animals with no one niche, caught between our animality and those symbolic, conceptual, technical systems of our own making.[62] We are centaurs who refuse to acknowledge the animal half, who repress and deny the facts of our embodiment, our fragility, and our finitude. And, as any number of thinkers have noted in their respective ways (from Freud to Heidegger, from Bataille to Brown and Becker), the human difference that arguably underwrites this centaur condition is exactly our awareness of death. This awareness will remain, alongside a heightened consciousness of embodiment and fragility, in any alternative social arrangement after the other surplus repressions and exploitative arrangements have been overcome. This awareness is central to any substantively utopian longing. But while high modernist dogma reifies this doubleness as division or opposition, after Descartes—who drew on a much longer tradition, rooted in Hellenistic Christianity and its Gnostic variants opposing (male) soul to (female) body, spirit to matter, culture to nature, and finally mind to body—we must embrace our doubleness.

How can we collectively live our continuities with non-human natures and Nature, and—insofar as we must also act in our specifically human capacity—repair the damage we've wrought on those natures and Nature through striving to repair them? This is the challenge, and the broader ethico-political stakes, for any degrowth or decelerationist ecosocialism.

And while I have intermittently drawn, here, on the broader existentialist tradition, it should be noted that this same modernist dogma informed the work of postwar existentialists such as Jean-Paul Sartre who arguably misinterpreted Heidegger, as well as an earlier phenomenological tradition, by rendering the world into which human beings are thrown as a dead and alien one: while this is in keeping with the long tradition of Cartesian rationalism, it resonates with the experience of late moderns who live in a "world of artifacts" exactly because "our experience of nature is restricted to contact with artifacts," as Erazim Kohák recognized. The postwar existentialists reified secondary alienation.[63]

The Critical Aquarians, very much shaped by a nascent awareness of the ecological crisis and our estrangement from nature, critically revised existentialism, and its phenomenological inheritance, alongside psychoanalysis, outlining something like an ecological existentialism—a position that insisted on our simultaneous continuity and discontinuity with the natural world, of which we are still a part. Rather than strong anthropocentrism, radical social constructionism, or naïve primitivism, any substantively ecosocialist politics must start from this position; just as any genuinely radical political project will aim to eliminate secondary alienation so that we can wrestle with the primary kind.

Jameson's Heideggerian Marxist reflections on Platonov's anti-modernist modernism arguably develop his more compelling, if implicit, insights into Boorman's *Zardoz*; that early essay certainly deserves some recognition as an inaugural effort in the theorist's sustained engagement with utopian (and dystopian) science fiction narratives. But unlike those later critical theorizations of utopia, whereby Jameson strives to rehabilitate a decidedly Promethean modernist impulse after trumpeting our postmodern condition throughout the Eighties and Nineties, his early review at least registers, in its attention to the film's kaleidoscopic collapse of period styles and registers, the new postmodern sensibility he would outline in his later work. Here was a missed opportunity, since the Critical Aquarian constellation of thinkers, writers, and activists out of which *Zardoz* represented a substantively countercultural postmodernism that deserves reexamination.

The primary question that united disparate thinkers from Brown, Illich, and Mies to Le Guin and the young Boorman was: How to exit the dead end of industrial modernism and its legitimating fictions—utilitarianism, Prometheanism, productivism and its ecocidal dreams of endless growth, secular immortality, and total control—in the face of interrelated material, ecological, and spiritual crises without sliding into the reactionary antimodernism that, for example, led certain disillusioned Western intellectuals to embrace the Iranian revolution at the end of the Seventies? While the urgency of the crises has increased a hundredfold since the 1970s, the question remains unanswered.

CODA: LETTERS FROM ANOTHER KIND OF UTOPIA

What first struck me about *Zardoz* and what remains are the images. It is, I have argued, a useful lens for delineating an early Seventies-era intellectual and imaginative constellation, a degrowth or decelerationist segment of a counterculture too often monolithically reduced to its techno-utopian or its individualist elements. Laying the question of whether Boorman made a great, good, or bad film aside—*Zardoz* is all three at once—his phantasmagoria is the dream of a certain moment, lending cryptic, sublime, and ridiculous forms to certain fears and wishes circulating through the "advanced" capitalist world in a period of transition. Like his Soviet contemporaries Andrei Tarkovsky and Sergei Parajanov, who similarly contested the state socialist flavor of hypermodernism by way of science fiction and folklore, Boorman selectively draws on the legacies of artistic modernism and its techniques for his own ends. *Zardoz* is, for example, very much organized around the visual conceit of a crystal, since the Tabernacle is contained in a crystal. While the film's comically iconic opening scenes, with stone head in Outlands, proceed through a series of wide-shot panoramic views redolent of landscape painting in a post-apocalyptic register, the film shifts into its characteristically crystalline mode once Zed breaches the Vortex.

From that point onward, the mise-en-scène is accordingly kaleidoscopic rather than sequential. Instead of quick cuts and sudden juxtapositions, we get frames within frames within frames, as Boorman collapses what could be a montage sequence of cut-image-cut into baroque and disorienting wide shots, apotheosized in Zed's examination under the probing hands (or AI-enhanced minds) of his new Eternal overlords after his first jarring appearance among them. We can see different figures—from Zed on the table to Eternals Consuella and May, who appear free floating even as they are supposedly examining their captive, to the regenerating bodies of the Eternals suspended, as if flying, in a synthetic amniotic fluid behind glass—engaged in different actions at different scales. It isn't just this surfeit of images that distinguishes the film, as certain critics suggested at the time, but the way Boorman renders sequential action as fractured simultaneity. The linear movement of progressive time, including the dialectical linearity of montage, has been flattened into a confused and blinking virtual world that suggests nothing so much as the cyberspace that was yet to come in 1974. It is as if Boorman acknowledges the irony of using film—a mechanically reproducible form of visual media that defines the modern period—to interrogate techno-modernism through an implosive visual language that cannibalizes much of film history. The only point when we see sequential time dramatized, in a deliberately overblown stop-motion montage, is during the film's coda. And there are no more arresting images in Boorman's film than these final ones.

In a film that consistently refuses montage until this penultimate point—after Zed and Consuella flee into the wreckage of the Zardoz head, after the collapse of the Vortex, refashioned as cave—Boorman presents his viewers with a time lapse montage of this reconstituted family's life cycle. From the couple, Zed and

Consuella, to a slightly older couple that includes a pregnant Consuella, to that same couple with a new child to an older child and finally the adult child who departs, the sequence concludes with the same couple reduced to their skeletal remains, hand bones clenched together, still (See Fig.17). Perhaps in implicit rebuke to the grand visions of historical progress that animated the nineteenth and twentieth centuries—when Progress and its utilitarian calculus were used by various regimes across the political spectrum to justify mass death in the present for the secular immortality to come—the film dramatizes the one unavoidably linear trajectory and its telos through what was once hailed as the most revolutionary-progressive film forms: montage.

This scene also presents the viewer with a reductio ad absurdum of the nuclear family as an insular dead end, especially when we consider that May, upon the dissolution of the Tabernacle and the Vortex, led a band of those now-mortal Eternals who opted to live their finite lives, rather than die, into the Outlands with the express purpose of building a new society alongside the Brutals. While this new dispensation remains offscreen, like some negative invocation of utopian possibility, in the film, Boorman (and Stair) provide more detail in their novelization, beginning with the end of the Vortex:

> This artificial Paradise, inset in the real world, making
> its surroundings the poorer because of its presence, had
> been swamped, flooded back into the Outlands. Now all
> the goodness that had been artfully stored here would be
> redistributed back into the places from which it had been
> stolen. May and her women would set out.[64]

Implicit in this extended novelistic account of the artificial paradise's "goodness" redistributed back into the "places from which" it was "stolen" is that broad anti-colonial sentiment that pervades the narrative, which Boorman here more explicitly links to ecological concerns—specifically the theory of uneven ecological exchange according to which high technology and the entire "imperial mode of living" is predicated on the exploitation and expropriation of the Outlands by a neocolonial core. May and her band are giving back what they stole while aiming to live as equals with the Brutals within the limits figured by the mortality they embrace in embracing the end of the Tabernacle and Vortex.

But what does ecosocial restitution look like in this case and on a devastated Earth? This is an Earth whose devastation stems from the Eternals' technosphere—gated communities behind invisible shields, organized under the auspices of A.I. governance, genetically engineered Immortals with replaceable bodies, a human zoo managed for maximum extraction beyond the walls, policed by an anti-gravity "god" ship. And lest we forget, this technology was first developed to flee the earth: "another dead end."[65] In an uncanny echo of our present-day "Long Termists," it was to secure the long-term survival of human civilization—at least for a certain sort of human being—against immediate and long term existential threats that this Immortalist order was established.

So, which of these technologies and techniques can May and her women repurpose in a sustainable and egalitarian way in the Outlands? Aside from the Eternals' ersatz immortality, ended by Zed, what technologies must they dismantle? And keeping the biophysical limits of a damaged planet in mind, what kinds of new collective self-limitation, and collective abundance, will characterize this new arrangement, as May and her band embrace birth, alongside death, in struggling to birth another society? These questions are even more pertinent now amidst general biospheric collapse, when the ruling classes of the global north, and their court ideologues, fantasize about decoupling from a natural world that always seems to include vast swathes of wretched humanity, and fleeing to the stars. While we do not want to junk the modern world or its infrastructures in their entirety, what do we salvage and how might we reconfigure various traditions and modes of being together in a way that allows for human and non-human flourishing on a finite planet? What does Ivan Illich's convivial technology look like? Or a degrowth socialism without austerity of the Malthusian sort? While this degrowth or—more accurately—decelerationist ecosocialism should and must draw on the modern revolutionary tradition, from council communism to social ecology, democratic self-governance and socialism, broadly understood, are not only the benevolent legacies of the modern era, like antibiotics. These political forms can also be found in the long, premodern history of human social organization, from paleolithic primitive communism to the admittedly imperfect polis to the Iroquois confederation of communes, among other, older forms of collective life. As opposed to the monoculture of capitalist modernity, ancient human history is a polycultural quilt of traditions that we must reinvent—as David Graeber and David Wengrow contend—after modernity.[66] Postmodernism in this sense is a radical traditionalism.

The Future according to Robert Crumb. (For his Historical vision, see p. 34.)

What might such a substantive postmodernism look like? Imagine a socio-technical order that mixed small towns or cities, built on the model of the medieval European commune or the Iroquois village, integrated into their bioregions, surrounded by belts of farmland, organized along the agro-ecological lines that blend traditional and contemporary modes of farming. Imagine that farmland surrounded by wilderness, which could include pasturage and pastoralism alongside a constellation of more-than-human lifeworlds. Imagine a decentralized renewable power grid and a centralized system of computers—perhaps, if energetically viable—subject to collective human imperatives and used solely in the service of eco-human ends coordinating the action of these various communes, when such coordination is necessary, after the elimination of personal digital devices and algorithmic post-political management. Imagine a mixture of animal power for transportation and agriculture, alongside bicycles and even high-speed trains—when necessary—and dirigibles floating against a clearer sky, after exhaust and light pollution, after the petro-automobile complex, after advertising, after exchange-value and its cancerous forms of development.

"But why?" ask our dogmatic hypermodernists. "To draw any line or to set any limit is arbitrary: If clean water or antibiotics, why not cryogenics or human-machine fusion of the Tabernacle sort?"

Putting aside the many ways that today's self-anointed elites use these ideological fantasies to mystify the workings of our catabolic capitalist order, this specious reasoning forecloses exactly those acts of judgment that define human reason: drawing lines and setting limits. These would-be human supremacists would instead cede our precious autonomy to "autonomous technology" and an inhuman idea of material development as an end in itself. One criterion for such judgments, outlined by Illich and others, is a technological order that serves genuinely human ends. We could further expand this aim to encompass creaturely and broadly ecological aims so that human ends never again compromise non-human lifeworlds, as we have done during the era of industrial capitalism.

Such a mix of "high" and "low" technology—a term I use capaciously to include narrowly technical structures and institutional arrangements—similarly shocks our hypermodernist ideologues, for partly aesthetic reasons, still looking forward to the uniform space-age technosphere envisioned in Kubrick's *2001*.

The goal is a human-scale and Earth-appropriate technics. Such a vision also offends modernist political ideologies in its mixture of centralization and decentralization, for example, and its implicit insistence on another ethos. Because such a project will require new norms and forms of life alongside transformed material structures, as the Critical Aquarians understood over fifty years ago.

Zed gets it and gets that he has no place in this new world:

If they were not all wiped out, they would have a hard
winter to survive alone; a brief time before the birth of
their children; then greater risk as they would be doubly
vulnerable. But some would not bear children, and they all
had had two hundred years of study and exercise to prepare
them for this time... Zed envied them. They would be the
first to land from this ship. The first explorers to set foot on
a new Earth.[67]

Inverting the pop-modernist cliché of space exploration as final frontier and upending the male-dominated project of an extraterrestrial exit from what some call, in a terminological fit of hubris, our "Anthropocene" Earth, we are instead presented with a band of women looking to rediscover and repair their old home. Marsha Kinder read in Boorman's depiction of the Vortex, seemingly dominated by women leaders such as May and Consuella, a misogyny that undercut his critique of technological utopias, as she notes:

When Friend releases the monster within him and rebels
against the utopia, he shouts: "The Vortex is an obscenity,
I hate all women". Suddenly we realize that the Vortex is an

image associated with female sexuality and that the women seem to be in control.[68]

But while Friend's rebellion ends in his begging Zed for immediate death, May and her cohort of women opt for a new, albeit finite, life, founding an alternative community that retains the matriarchal structure of the Vortex while jettisoning the rest. After fulfilling his role as sperm donor, Zed notably has no role or place in this new community, which suggests nothing so much as the eco-feminist visions of theorists such as Maria Mies and Carolyn Merchant or novelists like Ursula Le Guin.

Ursula Le Guin's "The Ones Who Walk Away from Omelas"—a short story published in October 1973—is a relevant Critical Aquarian intertext insofar as Le Guin rejects programmatic utopianism while maintaining a commitment to radical social transformation. The story's narrator describes a seeming utopia called Omelas in a self-reflexive way only to reveal that the Omelans' universal felicity depends on the perpetual degradation of a child kept in a grimy basement out of view, but not out of mind. Most Omelans visit this generic scapegoat of a child, sitting in its own excrement; they rationalize this suffering as the cost of the happiness, freedom, equality, and abundance they all enjoy as Omelans (all save one).[69]

Le Guin reveals the sacrificial impetus behind a utilitarian logic that ostensibly seeks to maximize the good of the majority—usually defined as the maximization of pleasure for the maximum number of people—even if that requires the institutionalized, if unseen, brutalization of a minority (of one in this case) as a means to an end; this scenario also mirrors the anti-colonial parable inscribed in the relationship between the Vortex and the Outlands. Le Guin's parable offers a rejoinder to what she calls the Euclidean or programmatic utopias that define the Western tradition from Plato through Thomas More to orthodox Marxism.

Like the imperfect and ambiguous utopia imagined on the planet Annares in Le Guin's *The Dispossessed*, her science fiction novel of the next year, and insofar as she depicts a substantively utopian impulse—directed against static utopias organized according to scientific principles rather than necessarily imperfect political struggles—it is found in the few Omelans who walk away from their "artificial paradise," or as Le Guin herself later articulated her position:

> Utopia has been Euclidean, it has been European, and it has been masculine. I am trying to suggest, in an evasive, distrustful, untrustworthy fashion, and as obscurely as I can, that our final loss of faith in that radiant sandcastle may enable our eyes to adjust to a dimmer light and in it perceive another kind of utopia. As this utopia would not be euclidean, European, or masculinist, my terms and images in speaking of it must be tentative and seem peculiar. Victor Turner's antitheses of structure and communitas are useful to my attempt to think about it: structure in society, in his terms, is cognitive, communitas existential; structure provides a model, communitas a potential; structure classifies, communitas reclassifies; structure is expressed in legal and political institutions, communitas in art and religion.[70]

I would also add, reading Le Guin's essay against her earlier story, that "communitas" is primarily the collective human process or action of rupture, creation, and the perpetual work of perennially imperfect recreation and maintenance that follows. Rather than in Omelas or some already existing place outside the city limits, Le Guin locates "utopia" in the ones who walk away or, more precisely, in their walking away — in their rejection of the Omelan status quo, in their exit, and finally, in their implied urge to build a new lifeworld, like May's new community in the Outlands.

Here is an example of natality—the human capacity for rupture and new beginnings, a collective non-biological elaboration of the birthing process that nonetheless bridges both halves of the centaur—most fully theorized by Hannah Arendt. While death forms the natural and existential horizon for all human beings, it is in the fact of our birth—which Heidegger or some of his followers negatively characterized as thrownness—that Arendt locates a distinctively human capacity for new beginnings.

Arendt synthesizes natural and social determinations in her account of an underdetermined human condition, as opposed to a fixed human nature. We are conditioned, on the most fundamental level, by the facts of birth and death and a survival imperative rooted in our corporeality and the historically specific biosphere through which we evolved and of which we are a part. These conditions connect us to the earth and all other forms of terrestrial creaturely life. But, after our centaur condition, we also build a world distinct from, yet dependent on, Earth that similarly shapes us as we shape it: "In addition to the conditions under which life is given to man on earth, and partly out of them, men constantly create their own, self-making conditions, which their human origin and their variability notwithstanding, possess the same conditioning power as natural things."[71]

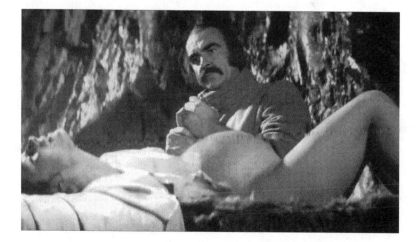

With this model of natality in mind, let's note how Zed's gift of death also includes the gift of birth—and all the gifts of embodied finitude—although Zed is pictured as mostly useless in this instance, standing to the side in a posture of mute, impotent encouragement as his companion pushes through the pain. Consuella's pregnancy (see Fig. 19) and delivery are the precondition for her unnamed son and this unnamed son's departure—in implicit rebuke to Zed and any aspiration to patrilineal or dynastic continuity—perhaps for May's new world. And that new world, organized along non-normative if not explicitly matriarchal lines, begins with the multiple pregnancies of her almost entirely female band. Against futurist feminist Shulamith Firestone, the "solution" to patriarchy is not the automation of the birth process but the transformation of eco-social relations such that birth (and death) are not horrible things to be denied, abolished, or transcended.

This sequence precedes and initiates the final montage sequence—both set to the rhythmic, simultaneously stirring and dirge-like Allegretto movement of Beethoven's Symphony No. 7 in A major, op. 92 that binds them together—and its two endpoints. Musical passages from Symphony No. 7 recur throughout the film, alongside alternating snatches of incidental and synthesizer music, arranged by early music pioneer David Munrow. Boorman strives to create a visual analog for an extended piece of music, using recurrent leitmotifs and variations to mark thematic continuities. This approach reaches a condensed apotheosis in the final few minutes of the film: the ostensibly linear progression that constitutes the film's finale is, on closer examination, a contrapuntal play of motifs.

One such motif reaches its endpoint in the death and disintegration of Zed and Consuella, foregrounding finitude and its acceptance as the existential horizon of creaturely being, particularly on the individual level. But the other endpoint—the growth and departure of the child turned adult, perhaps for May's utopia limited—is a necessary complement to that finitude, which expands and negates — expands because it negates — the narrowly biological fact of birth: "The miracle that saves the world, the realm of human affairs, from its normal, "natural" ruin is ultimately the fact of natality, in which the faculty of action is ontologically rooted. It is, in other words, the birth of new men and the new beginning, the action they are capable of by virtue of being born."[72]

We are born, live, and die in time, as both products and makers of our times. We persist beyond the span of an individual life in the form of our collective arrangements and traditions. The "birth of new men and the new beginning" ensure both the continuity of those traditions and the possibility of ruptures or revolutions. Traditions long dead, even the traditions of the vanquished, can be resurrected or recreated by new people in their own time, according to their own needs. Perhaps this is the meaning of the final image (See Fig. 20) in John Boorman's hieroglyphic spectacle: a rusty, cobwebbed six-shooter, apparently Zed's, hangs suspended in front of a cave wall stained with handprints. While the absurdly antiquated gun—an emblem of the ways high technological development intersects with war-making—suggests, in a hopeful way, a future in which systematic extermination is a relic, the handprints evoke the prehistoric cave painting at Lascaux. Does Boorman here imply that the events of the film, ostensibly set in the far future world of 2293, occur in some prehistoric past? Even as the film clearly builds on the disastrous twentieth century and its late-stage dystopian fears, here is a final imagistic rebuke to dominant ideas of homogeneous and linear time or Progress.

More than cyclical time or the Nietzschean "eternal recurrence of the same," the handprints attest to human finitude, continuity, and the possibility of re-creation across qualitatively different times and temporalities. It is both the limit conditions of our time-bound human, or creaturely, condition and the sheer contingency of history, human and natural, that allows for new beginnings, even among the ruins.

ENDNOTES

1. Boorman, John and Bill Stair. *Zardoz*. New York: Signet, 1974, 10. I use John Boorman's and Bill Stair's novelization of Boorman's *Zardoz* screenplay for all direct quotations throughout this book. According to Boorman—in his short preface to the 1974 novel—he originally wrote the film as a novel and then gradually revised it as a shooting script. Boorman then decided to restore the story to novel form, with the assistance of Stair, who worked on the film, drawing on the earlier versions of the tale.

2. *Ibid.*, "Preface." The "Celtic twilight" here refers to Boorman's home in County Wicklow, Ireland, where he shot the film.

3. Hoyle, Brian. *The Cinema of John Boorman*. Plymouth: The Scarecrow Press Inc. 2012, 96.

4. Boorman and Stair, *Zardoz*, 94.

5. Hoyle, *The Cinema of John Boorman*, 102.

6. Kinder, Marsha. "Zardoz [Review]." *Film Quarterly*, Vol. 27, 58.

7. Boorman, John. "Zardoz and John Boorman." By Phillip Strick. *Sight and Sound*. Vol. 43, No. 2 (Spring 1974), 77.

8. Fisher, Mark. *Ghosts of My Life: Writings on Depression, Hauntology and Lost Futures*. London: Zero Books, 2014. *Zardoz*, in blending experimental with popular aesthetic techniques, in many ways exemplifies what Mark Fisher dubbed "popular modernism." In Fisher's account, "popular modernism," or artistic experimentation,

characterized the mass cultural production of the still capitalist yet more social democratic West of the sixties and seventies, as we can see in BBC television serial *Sapphire and Steel* or the popular music of the time, ranging from prog rock to post-punk, or indeed films like *Zardoz*. Fisher sees in these cultural experiments the last repositories of those twentieth-century utopian aspirations—which he links to modernist socialism—or futures lost under the neoliberal settlement of the 1980s and beyond, when postmodern "retromania" supplanted both political and cultural experimentation in keeping with Margaret Thatcher's infamous claim that there is no alternative to capitalism. That said, the "lost futures" that we might discern in *Zardoz* and so many of the other, comparable works from the time are very much interrogations, and often outright rejections, of the modernist futurism that Fisher mourns, even as these works outline alternatives outside Promethean techno-utopianism, capitalist and socialist alike.

9. Frase, Peter. *Four Futures: Life After Capitalism*. London and New York: Verso, 2016. For an extended engagement with Frase's, on my part, see Galluzzo, Anthony. "Utopia as Method, Social Science Fiction, and the Flight From Reality." *boundary 2*, August 25, 2017. https://www.boundary2.org/2017/08/anthony-galluzzo-utopia-as-method-social-science-fiction-and-the-flight-from-reality/.

10. Boorman, John. *Zardoz*. Twentieth Century Fox. 1974.

11. Jameson, Fredric. "History and the death wish: *Zardoz* as open form." *Jump Cut: A Review of Contemporary Media*. No. 3, (1974), 8.

12. Boorman, John. "Moments of Transcendence: An Interview with John Boorman." By Declan McGrath. *Cinéaste*. Vol. 40, No. 2 (Spring 2015), 35.

13. Boorman, John. "Zardoz and John Boorman," 75.

14. Boorman, "Moments of Transcendence," 33.

15. Boorman, "Zardoz and John Boorman," 75.

16. *Ibid*.

17. Turner, Fred. *From Counterculture to Cyberculture: Stewart Brand, the Whole Earth Network, and the Rise of Digital Utopianism*. Chicago and London: University of Chicago Press, 2008.

18. Miller, John Steven. *The Seventies Now: Culture as Surveillance*. Durham: Duke University Press, 1999, 16.

19. Tierney, Matt. *Dismantlings: Words Against Machines in the American Long Seventies*. Ithaca and London: Cornell University Press, 2019, 25.

20. Ibid., 27.

21. Levine, Yasha. *Surveillance Valley: The Secret Military History of The Internet*. London: Icon Books, 2019.

22. See the chapter entitled "Technological Politics" in Winner, Langdon. *Autonomous Technology: Technics-out-of-Control as a Theme in Political Thought*. Cambridge, Mass.: MIT Press, 1977.

23. Boorman and Stair, *Zardoz*, 39.

24. *Ibid.*, 104.

25. Tierney, *Dismantlings*, 26.

26. Sully, Justin. "On the Cultural Projection of Population Crisis: The Case of *The Omega Man*." *Criticism*. Vol. 58, No. 1 (Winter 2016), 100.

27. Robertson, Thomas. *The Malthusian Moment: Global Growth and the Birth of American Environmentalism*. Piscataway: Rutgers University Press, 2012, 158.

28. See Chapter 3—"The Whole Earth Catalogue as Information Technology'—in Turner, *From Counterculture to Cyberculture*.

29. Boorman and Stair, *Zardoz*, 104.

30. Cayley, David. *The Rivers North of the Future: The Testament of Ivan Illich as Told to David Cayley*. Toronto: House of Anansi Press, 2005, 16–17.

31. Hardin, Garrett. "Living on a Lifeboat." *BioScience*. 24, No. 10 (October 1974): 561–568.

32. Lovelock, James. *Gaia: A New Look at Life on Earth*. Oxford: Oxford University Press, 1979, 12. Lovelock, a Quaker and one-time NASA scientist, was a fascinating and contradictory figure who, late in his very long life, ironically came to embrace geoengineering and AI superintelligence as the only hope for saving the biosphere. I hesitate to draw a line between his enthusiasm for cybernetics and this later turn. While cybernetics, a term coined by computer scientist Norbert Wiener, was initially focused on machines, it encompasses self-correcting feedback loops and self-regulation in any and all systems, including ecosystems. Of course, the problem is exactly how living systems get collapsed into mechanical systems without any attention paid to qualitative distinctions. And much Sixties- and Seventies-era cybernetic or systems theory sought to address these qualitative

distinctions, as we can see in the work of Chilean biologists Humberto Maturana and Francisco Varela or anthropologist Gregory Bateson. For example, while "autopoiesis" is usually classified as a cybernetic concept, Dorion Sagan contends, in his recent introduction to a text he coauthored with his mother, Lynn Margulis: "Gaia itself may not be best described as a reactive, cybernetic system, but rather an anticipative, autopoietic one. Autopoiesis (auto:'self': poiesis; 'making') refers to a system—living matter—that is self-reflexive, self-oriented, self-producing." Note the qualitative distinction between living and dead matter here, and, implicitly, between living systems and human artifacts. Critical Aquarianism—and the longer romantic tradition—is not against "science"; its representatives instead advocate the holistic and relational scientific approach exemplified by ecology, Gaia theory, and Margulis's work on symbiosis; Margulis, Lynn and Dorion Sagan. *Gaia and Philosophy.* Great Britain: Ignota Books, 2023, 9.

33. Boorman and Stair, *Zardoz*, 79.

34. Boorman, John. *Adventures of a Suburban Boy*. London: Faber and Faber, 2003, 204.

35. Commoner, Barry. "The Technological Flaw," in *Notes for the Future: An alternative history of the past decade*. Ed. Robin Clarke. New York: Universe Books, 1975, 99. See also: Commoner, Barry. *The Closing Circle: Nature, Man, and Technology*. New York: Dover, 1971, 2020.

36. Hoff, Derek S. *The State and the Stork: The Population Debate and Policy Making in US History*. Chicago and London: University of Chicago Press, 2012, 191.

37. Kallis, Giorgos. *Limits: Why Malthus Was Wrong and Why Environmentalists Should Care*. Stanford: Stanford University Press, 2019, 33.

38. Boorman and Stair, *Zardoz*, 51.

39. Hägglund, Martin. *This Life: Secular Faith and Spiritual Freedom*. New York: Pantheon 2020, 68.

40. Brown, Norman O. *Life Against Death: The Psychoanalytical Meaning of History*. Middletown: Wesleyan University Press, 1959, 1985, 104.

41. Ibid., 91.

42. Ibid., 308.

43. Becker, Ernest. *The Denial of Death*. New York: Free Press, 1973, 265.

44. Arendt, Hannah. *The Human Condition*. Chicago and London: The University of Chicago Press, 1958, 1998, 6.

45. Cayley, David. *Ivan Illich: An Intellectual Journey*. University Park: The Pennsylvania State University Press, 2021, 126.

46. Entropy as concept, theme, and metaphor runs throughout Pynchon's work from his early short story "Entropy" through his novels *V*, *The Crying of Lot 49*, *Gravity's Rainbow* and beyond.

47. Kallis, *Limits*, 92.

48. Boorman, "John Boorman and Zardoz," 76–77.

49. Boorman and Stair, *Zardoz*, 124.

50. Kinder, "Zardoz [Review]," 56.

51. Jameson, "History and The Death Wish," 1.

52. Boorman, "Moments of Transcendence," 33.

53. Jameson, "History and The Death Wish," 9.

54. Hornborg, Alf. 2001. *Nature, Society, and Justice in the Anthropocene: Unraveling the Money-Energy-Technology Complex*. Cambridge: Cambridge University Press, 2019, 100.

55. Jameson, "History and The Death Wish," 5.

56. Ibid., 6.

57. Godwin outlines a science fictional scenario in the final chapter of his visionary 1793 perfectibilist *Enquiry Considering Political Justice*—specifically in response to the challenges posed by population growth and resource limits in the advanced agrarian economic conditions of late eighteenth-century England. According to the young Godwin, the inevitable triumph of Reason (and anarchist "political simplicity") will lead to both immortality and a more rational, sexless condition (as sex, equated with reproduction, will be rendered superfluous under this immortal and super-rationalist dispensation). It was this Godwin that Malthus was primarily responding to in his first *Essay on Population* (1798), although Godwin had retreated from his proto-Singularitarianism, if not his radical political convictions, by the later 1790s as evinced by *St. Leon*, a Gothic novel that details the pain and horrors experienced by the titular alchemist who discovers the secrets of eternal life (and power) by way of his alchemical activities. This

critical interrogation of Prometheanism, including Godwin's own earlier Promethean convictions, also shaped his daughter's *Frankenstein*. Godwin's and Malthus's respective models of historical progress weren't so different in the end, as I argue in Galluzzo, Anthony, "The Singularity in the 1790s toward a Prehistory of the Present with William Godwin and Thomas Malthus." *boundary 2*. Sept. 17, 2018. https://www.boundary2.org/2018/09/galluzzo/.

58. Adorno, Theodor. "Aldous Huxley and Utopia" in *Prisms*. Cambridge, Mass.: MIT Press, 1967, 115.

59. Ibid., 114.

60. Jameson, Fredric. "Utopia, Modernism, and Death" in *The Seeds of Time*. New York: Columbia University Press, 110.

61. Nersessian, Anahid. *Utopia, Limited: Romanticism and Adjustment*. Cambridge, Mass.: Harvard University Press, 2015.

62. Evernden, Neil. *The Natural Alien: Humankind and Environment*. Toronto, University of Toronto Press, 1985, 1993, 122–123.

63. Kohák, Erazim. *The Embers and The Starts: a philosophical inquiry into the moral sense of nature*. Chicago and London: University of Chicago Press, 1984, 13.

64. Boorman and Stair, *Zardoz*, 122.

65. Ibid., 104.

66. Graeber, David and David Wengrow. *The Dawn of Everything: A New History of Humanity*. New York: Farrar, Staruss, and Giroux, 2021.

67. Boorman and Stair, *Zardoz*, 123.

68. Kinder, "Zardoz (Review), 56.

69. Le Guin, Ursula. "The Ones Who Walk Away from Omelas" in *The Wind's Twelve Quarters: Stories*. New York, Harper and Row, 1976.

70. Le Guin, Ursula. "A Non-Euclidean View of California as a Cold Place to Be" in *Always Coming Home* (Author's Expanded Edition). New York: Library of America, 2019, 711–712.

71. Arendt, *The Human Condition*, 9.

72. Ibid., 247.

CULTURE, SOCIETY & POLITICS

Contemporary culture has eliminated the concept and public
figure of the intellectual. A cretinous anti-intellectualism
presides, cheer-led by hacks in the pay of multinational
corporations who reassure their bored readers that there is no
need to rouse themselves from their stupor. Zer0 Books knows
that another kind of discourse — intellectual without being
academic, popular without being populist — is not only possible
but already flourishing. Zer0 is convinced that in the unthinking,
blandly consensual culture in which we live, critical and
engaged theoretical reflection is more important
than ever before.
If you have enjoyed this book, why not tell other readers by
posting a review on your preferred book site.
You may also wish to
subscribe to our Zer0 Books YouTube Channel.

Color, Facture, Art and Design
Iona Singh
This materialist definition of fine art develops guidelines for
architecture, design, cultural studies, and ultimately, social change.
Paperback: 978-1-78099-629-5 ebook: 978-1-78099-630-1

Sweetening the Pill
or How We Got Hooked on Hormonal Birth Control
Holly Grigg-Spall
Has contraception liberated or oppressed women?
Sweetening the Pill breaks the silence on the dark side of hormonal
contraception.
Paperback: 978-1-78099-607-3 ebook: 978-1-78099-608-0

Why Are We the Good Guys?
Reclaiming Your Mind from the Delusions of Propaganda
David Cromwell
A provocative challenge to the standard ideology that Western
power is a benevolent force in the world.
Paperback: 978-1-78099-365-2 ebook: 978-1-78099-366-9

The Writing on the Wall
On the Decomposition of Capitalism and its Critics
Anselm Jappe, Alastair Hemmens
A new approach to the meaning of social emancipation.
Paperback: 978-1-78535-581-3 ebook: 978-1-78535-582-0

Neglected or Misunderstood
The Radical Feminism of Shulamith Firestone
Victoria Margree
An interrogation of issues surrounding gender, biology,
sexuality, work and technology, and the ways in which our
imaginations continue to be in thrall to ideologies of maternity
and the nuclear family.
Paperback: 978-1-78535-539-4 ebook: 978-1-78535-540-0

How to Dismantle the NHS in 10 Easy Steps (Second Edition)
Youssef El-Gingihy
The story of how your NHS was sold off and why you will have
to buy private health insurance soon. A new expanded second
edition with chapters on junior doctors' strikes and government
blueprints for US-style healthcare.
Paperback: 978-1-78904-178-1 ebook: 978-1-78904-179-8

Digesting Recipes
The Art of Culinary Notation
Susannah Worth
A recipe is an instruction, the imperative tone of the expert, but
this constraint can offer its own kind of potential. A recipe need
not be a domestic trap but might instead offer escape —
something to fantasise about or aspire to.
Paperback: 978-1-78279-860-6 ebook: 978-1-78279-859-0

Most titles are published in paperback and as an ebook.
Paperbacks are available in traditional bookshops. Both print
and ebook formats are available online.
Follow us at:
https://www.facebook.com/ZeroBooks
https://twitter.com/Zer0Books
https://www.instagram.com/zero.books

For video content, author interviews and more, please subscribe to our YouTube channel:

zer0repeater

Follow us on social media for book news, promotions and more:

Facebook: ZeroBooks

Instagram: @zero.books

X: @Zer0Books

Tik Tok: @zer0repeater